Startups & Self-care

THE POWER OF BUILDING A BUSINESS FROM A PLACE OF PASSION, PURPOSE AND PURITY OF INTENTION

MEGAN LARSEN

Published in Australia by Samhita
meganlarsen.com.au

National Library of Australia Publication Data
available via www.nla.gov.au

ISBN: 978-0-6484250-0-7

Printed in Australia

Cover design: Jacqui Porter, Northwood Green
Cover image: Mark Lane, Laneway Photos
Cover makeup: Samantha Powell
Interior design: Swish Design
Interior images: via shutterstock.com and the author

First Edition

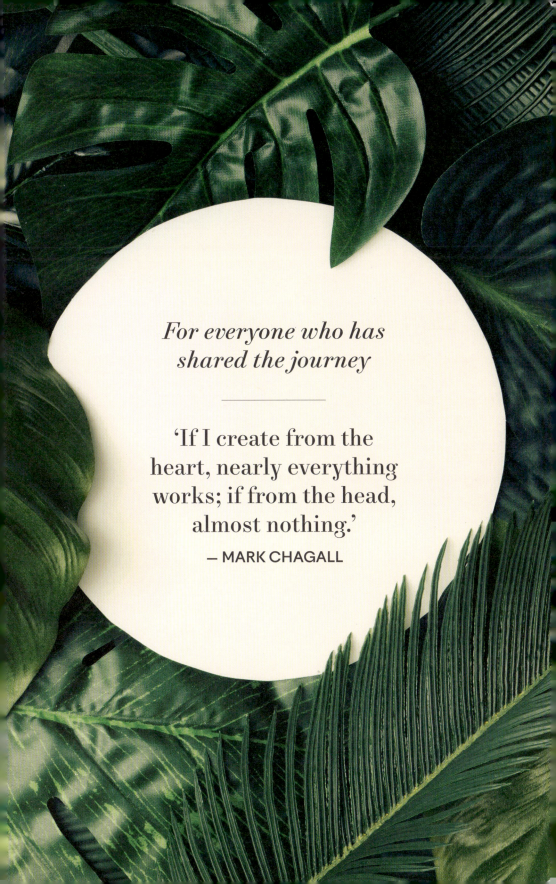

For everyone who has shared the journey

'If I create from the heart, nearly everything works; if from the head, almost nothing.'

— MARK CHAGALL

Contents

Foreword

ZOË FOSTER BLAKE

I knew of Sodashi before I met the founder, Megan.

But when I met her in person, during a press junket at Wolgan Valley in 2009, I *got it*. I wanted in. I heard the story, I believed the promise, I wanted to use ALL the products, and I *really* liked the woman driving it, and what she stood for. A good brand story and founder will do that.

Megan commands a room in the most subtle, magical fashion. She is charming, warm, funny and fun, but she is also verbally economic, has a breathtaking poker face, and thinks through EVERYTHING before she says it. She is a lady Yoda, basically. I feel like she knows what I'm thinking (or who I am and what I need to do in life) before I do. She is profoundly perceptive and sensitive with a tremendous read of character, and she does *naaaay* suffer fools.

Megan is not only an innovator of the natural skin care movement, she is a pioneer (higher up than an innovator, and with a better car spot) of organic skin care, chemical-free skin care and eco luxe. Before Sodashi came along, you had premium skin care, and you had organic skin care; the two didn't intersect, let alone party in sleek violet glass jars. Megan expertly merged the two, creating products that she herself wanted, and that didn't exist. She trusted her vision, and she did it all with scrupulous care, passion, love and the belief that what she was doing was the Right Thing. She did good work, and she did it bloody well.

Megan is prolific, extremely busy, and travels more than your average pilot, yet is somehow always calm, focused and mentally present. This is *not* the demeanour of a person who is overwhelmed and overextended, who is Doing Too Much, at the cost of her health, relationships and sanity. (Or in other words: the rest of us.)

It is *so clear* that Megan takes care of herself. She never misses a meditation (even at the expense of cocktails) and she recognises instantly when her inner introvert is waving the white flag, or her body needs a rest, and she responds accordingly. She channels her energy purposefully, and judiciously. It's both admirable and envy-inducing.

I mention this, because I believe *who* Megan is, how she does life, is the reason Sodashi is such a huge and global success. The products, treatments and team enjoy a flawless reputation, and people who love Sodashi REALLY LOVE Sodashi. (Is cult too strong a word?)

But Megan is not just the heart of Sodashi, she is an active force in the company, leading and educating her team, instilling purpose and vision into the company, developing new products, and relentlessly seeking to learn more and challenge herself. She has learned how to walk the line between creative visionary, and running the day-to-day business, with grace.

Oh, yeah, *and she changed my life forever.* It was Megan, who, during one of our regular wine-laden catch-ups, where, as I attempted to persuade a woman with an internationally acclaimed skin care line into making a new product simply because I wanted it to exist (now a Go-To product), she smiled and replied: why don't *you* make it?

The idea of creating a skin care line had never entered my mind. Megan saw the opportunity objectively and clearly, and encouraged me generously, and wholeheartedly, offering me not only invaluable, proven startup advice, but through her network, a brilliant formulator and our fantastic MD.

Five years later and we're valued at over $500 billion.

That's a lie, but look, we're doing great. We've just launched into US Sephora, and there would be no Go-To if Megan hadn't planted the seed that day, and then watered it enough to get that seedling to shoot up.

And now YOU, lucky ol' you, have access to all the magic and wisdom in Megan's beautiful brain.

Any goose can launch a startup, there is zero barrier to entry these days, but that doesn't mean it will be successful, or sustainable, or enjoyable. *We all need help.* We all need advice. We're all learning, all the time. And getting insight from a successful founder with decades of professional experience on how to launch and maintain a company, and do it in a way that is meaningful, and ideally, profitable, while not losing yourself or your health along the way, well, that's not nothing.

Enjoy Megan's story, enjoy your journey, and *remember to moisturise.*

Zoë Foster Blake,
Author, founder of Go-To

Introduction

'Startups and self-care? Those aren't words you see together very often.'

I'd just shared the title of the book I was writing—this book—with a friend. Her words immediately took me back 19 years, all the way to the beginning of my startup journey, and the years of scepticism I battled when people heard me put the words 'all-natural' and 'skin care' together.

While 'all-natural' is de rigueur in 2018, it simply wasn't a thing in 1999 when I founded Sodashi. I spent years convincing the market that skin care products made from the purest botanical and marine extracts could also be high performing and deliver noticeable and lasting results.

Would I now also need to educate the market that it *was* possible to be a startup founder who looked after themselves? And that in looking after yourself you would build a stronger company?

Well, if that's how things were going to pan out, I was up for it.

Then, just as I was finalising this manuscript, the results of research commissioned by KPMG Australia's High Growth Ventures practice[1] were released. The aim of the research was to investigate the link between the wellbeing of a founder and the success of their startup.

Amanda Price, head of the High Growth Ventures practice, stated:

> This research [was] born out of two key hypotheses. Firstly, a founder's ability to lead their business is a critical success factor that determines the fate of their startup. And secondly, that a founder's personal wellbeing, their physical and mental health, informs how they lead ... and build the culture necessary for a startup to succeed.

I certainly know the truth of those words.

I've spent 19 years growing Sodashi from humble beginnings in my kitchen to where it is today: an award-winning global entity.

As I write this, Sodashi's range of all-natural, high-performance skin care products has grown to over 80. We supply more than 70 luxury spas in more than 25 countries globally, including Four Seasons, Jumeirah and Emirates properties. And our most conservative estimates suggest more than three million people worldwide have experienced a Sodashi product.

In a journey that's featured countless challenges and are-you-kidding-me moments, I've always been aware that as a founder, my health, wellbeing and mindset were crucial to surviving the startup rollercoaster ride.

So it's no surprise that when I'm asked about the secret behind my longevity in the industry, and my ability to bring the same energy, passion and purpose to the business today that I did 19 years ago, I point to self-care.

[1] *Research into the wellbeing of startup founders and entrepreneurs* KPMG.com/au/highgrowthventures

'A founder's ability to lead their business is a critical success factor that determines the fate of their startup.'

— KPMG HIGH GROWTH VENTURES

It's a term that tends to conjure up images of health spas and wellness retreats—things I know few startup founders have time to indulge in. And while I believe those forms of self-care have their place, when I say 'self-care' I mean 'looking after myself physically, mentally, spiritually and emotionally'.

While that might sound like a lot of work, I can assure you it's not. You can do some simple things each day, week and month to recharge, refocus, and ensure you can give your startup the energy and resilience it needs from you.

There are the obvious things: eating well, exercising daily and getting good sleep. But there's also surrounding yourself with good people, as well as the one I'm most known for: meditation. (More on that later.)

· · ·

When I first started writing this book, I was willing to take on the load of selling the idea of self-care to startup owners. I was more than happy to be the voice speaking out against the 'go hard or go home' message so many startup owners adhere to and preach.

Fortunately, the release of the KPMG report showed me the mental shift is already happening. I don't need to *drive* the idea that looking after yourself is one of the greatest investments you can make in growing your startup. I just need to *support* it by showing how it's worked for me, Sodashi (as a business) and the Sodashi team.

So here's how this book is going to work.

I'll start by sharing the Sodashi story and the **major startup learnings** I've taken away from 19 years building and growing a business—one that involved pioneering a new concept the world wasn't quite ready for.

Then I'll discuss something I haven't seen too many founders talk about: the **tricky transition** we need to make when our startup crosses the threshold and becomes an established business.

After that we'll have a brief interlude where I share some of my **favourite quotes and mantras** and how I apply them to startup life. These are thoughts and ideas I return to frequently that keep my mind balanced and open in the face of challenges.

Finally, I'll talk about **self-care**, what it means to me, and what it should mean to you.

WHO THIS BOOK IS FOR

Anyone who's ever experienced a Sodashi skin care product will appreciate following the journey we've taken, from its humble beginnings in my kitchen to a global brand.

If you're driven by passion and purpose, and wondering what it looks like to turn those qualities into a thriving business, I hope this book will help answer many of the questions you have.

And if you're the founder of a startup or the owner of an established business who's wondering if there's an alternative to constantly feeling burnt out and overwhelmed, this book is *definitely* for you.

By the end of this book I want you to feel more supported on your business journey, and equipped to build yourself a simple and effective self-care mindset and routine. One that will boost your resilience, clear your mind and give you the space you need to:

- make great decisions
- be a great boss/leader
- form the quality relationships needed to make your startup a success.

If that all sounds good to you, turn the page and let's get started.

Startups

THE START

Where does the story of a startup really begin? Most people think it's with the idea for 'the thing'—the product or service you end up building your business around. But I believe most startup stories begin much earlier.

Mine began in my hometown in New Zealand.

People often ask me whether my entrepreneurial spirit is a result of nature or nurture. I always reply 'both'. While I was certainly naturally entrepreneurial, that side of me would have struggled to show its face if not for the example of my mother.

When I look back, I can see she was probably a little ahead of her time. (A trait I ended up taking into Sodashi.) She was this fiercely strong and independent woman doing whatever needed to be done to provide for her family and raise two kids by herself in the late '60s and '70s.

She was incredibly resourceful. Some would say she had a degree in life. She grew our fruit and vegetables, which would also be turned into jams, chutneys and preserves. She painted and wallpapered the house. She changed the washers on our taps when they leaked. And she was never shy when it came to changing a tyre on the car.

She even went to woodwork classes because she wanted to learn woodwork.

She also learnt pottery and went on to build a business with her craft, which was such a learning experience for me.

While my mother wasn't successful in teaching me how to change washers or work with wood, she raised me to be confident in my abilities and taught me the importance of backing yourself. She also instilled in me a belief that I could do anything I wanted to if I really put my mind to it. There was a saying she adapted for me: 'Come hell or high water I know you're going to do it, because that's what you want to do'.

And she led by example. It was incredibly inspiring to watch her slowly turn her pottery passion and hobby into a business— one that supported our household and allowed her to be there for my brother and me.

It wasn't easy work. She'd be in the potting shed at five in the morning, before we woke up, and then she'd come in and get us off to school before going back to work. After school she'd spend the afternoon with us, or sometimes we'd spend time talking with her in her potting shed. We'd have dinner, and then she often headed back to the potting shed when we were in bed.

When my friends came over after school they always wanted to go to the potting shed and watch Mum, fascinated by her work.

What I remember most is she was always there for us to listen to the highs and lows of our day.

I also remember my earliest lessons in resilience coming from my mother.

The town I grew up in was very earthquake prone. It's renowned for the huge earthquake in 1931 that changed much of Napier's landscape. Thankfully we didn't have earthquakes every day. But we always knew to expect them, particularly in February and March.

I remember several occasions where Mum filled her one cubic metre kiln with pots, fired it up, and then we'd have an earthquake. She'd never know what had happened to the pots until she could open the door the next morning. We all felt her anxiety as we waited for the kiln to be cool enough to open the door. Pots would often be stuck together, rendering them useless. It was devastating for my mum, a single mother raising two kids, as this was her only source of income.

But she never complained to us. Instead she seemed to realise it was all part of potting in an earthquake prone area, and she'd just get on with doing what she needed to do—remaking the pots she'd lost.

So while I believe the drive I have (which every budding entrepreneur needs) is hardwired into me, being raised in New Zealand by this amazing and adaptable woman gave me a rock-solid foundation of belief and an unshakeable resilience.

It's something I'm forever thankful for, as I've lost count of the times I've had to call on belief and resilience over the course of my entrepreneurial journey.

WHAT'S YOUR BACKSTORY?

If you've taken an entrepreneurial path, it might be interesting to reflect on when and where it all began. It might be the first time you were inspired to think outside the box. It might be when you first realised you had control over how your future could be.

When I dial into my backstory I can clearly see the seeds my mother planted when it came to turning my passion into my purpose, and my purpose into a career.

She also set high standards for herself and had great integrity. My mother couldn't tolerate a pot that wasn't centred or finished properly. She was a craftswoman. On countless occasions she'd take a piece off the wheel, or even after first firing, and throw it in the bin. If the pot hadn't been fired she would recycle the clay to make another pot. Occasionally she would make her 'seconds' available to her friends, but she'd never sell them at full price.

I have no doubt my mother was driven by passion and purpose when it all began 47 years ago. It was why she could get up at 5am, take breaks throughout the day to be our mum, and then return to potting when she'd put us to bed.

Did I sit there watching her pot and decide, 'One day I'm going to have my own business'? Absolutely not. But I did absorb the lessons that were on the table:

- You could succeed if you put your mind to something and gave it your positive attention.
- You could make a business from your passion and purpose.

I believe that when you understand your backstory and identify where your drive comes from, it really bolsters your resilience and gives you the fortitude to push through tough times. It also allows you to appreciate the great times.

———————— ● ● ● ————————

LEARNING

It's always interesting to hear what kind of relationship fellow entrepreneurial types had with school. And I'm never surprised when they say they didn't love it.

Beyond the social side of things, school certainly didn't work for me. I loved learning, but only about things I was interested in and could see a point to. For example, I didn't really understand the purpose of maths and so I struggled with it. But I loved commerce and had a good mind for it.

I was keen to leave school as soon as possible. But my mother insisted I get my High School Certificate and encouraged me to find a part-time job instead. So I took the general interest I had in cosmetics, headed into Napier, and walked around to all the pharmacies asking if they had any positions going. I got a call back from one and started working there after school a couple of nights a week. Eventually a full-time role became available and having attained my High School Certificate, it was time for me to enter the working world.

Given I had no inkling that starting a skin care range lay in my future, it's fascinating to look back at what I learned about skin care from working at that particular pharmacy.

The pharmacist was also known as a compounding chemist, which is the art and science of preparing personalised medications for patients. We did preparations for all sorts of skin ailments. I got to observe how they were made, how they worked, and how to make things in small batches.

It's also where I first learnt about sales. I had great success educating people about the right tone of lipstick for their colouring, what foundation would suit them best, and how to look after their skin. The various cosmetic houses knew a lot about selling through education and ran a series of two-day courses around skin and cosmetics. I attended all those courses and soaked up everything they taught.

When I was 18 I saw an ad in a magazine that said, 'Come to Sydney and study beauty therapy.' New Zealand had only one beauty therapy school at the time, and I was excited about the prospect of going to Sydney to study.

I consulted with my mum. She was nervous at the thought of her daughter 'crossing the ditch' to study, but she was so incredibly supportive, and I know in her heart she wanted me to expand and grow. So I made my first journey out of New Zealand to Sydney.

Interestingly, despite completing my studies in beauty therapy I never actually worked in the industry full-time. Instead, I was drawn to the hospitality industry. I enjoyed the opportunities, interesting work and real-world education I found there. Even though I was young, I knew what I liked and wanted to learn more of. And that drove where I went work-wise.

SYDNEY > PERTH > KUNUNURRA

In 1986, after spending time back in New Zealand to help my mum through a period of personal upheaval, I returned to Sydney where I was greeted by some friends.

'We're driving across the Nullarbor to Perth to go to the America's Cup,' they said. 'Want to come?'

There was nothing especially holding me to Sydney, so I said 'Sure. Why not?'

Being in Perth during the America's Cup was fun. I didn't know much about the city before moving there, but quickly got caught up in the energy and excitement, particularly around the area of Fremantle where the racing was taking place.

On my arrival, I started doing temporary office/admin/accounts work, and one of my assignments was with one of Kevin Parry's businesses. At the time Kevin Parry's yacht 'Kookaburra III' was racing to beat Alan Bond and defend the Cup, which he did successfully. (Unfortunately, Dennis Conner and his yacht 'Stars and Stripes' then went on to win the whole thing.) Still, it was exciting to be in an office surrounded by the spirit of competition, even if only for a couple of months.

When it was all over, and the excitement wound down, I felt it was time to explore the big wide land and state of Western Australia.

I'd been speaking to someone who'd worked 'up north' (as the northern part of Western Australia is known). I started looking into positions up there, and one came up in Broome. I applied, got the job with Western Resorts, and was all primed to experience the beautiful Cable Beach sunsets I'd heard so much about.

But alas it didn't happen. The company called me and said 'Oh, we've got a role we'd really like you to fill in Kununurra, so we need you to go there instead'.

Now, Kununurra is a small country town located in the extreme north of Western Australia, only 37 km from the Northern Territory. It's inland, so no beach sunsets, and to say it's 'remote' is a huge understatement.

Everything I'd learned so far about resilience got put to work in Kununurra.

I arrived in November 1987, in what's called 'the rainy season'. The rainy season features days where you have this intense cloud build-up with a combination of heat and humidity like nothing you've ever experienced, closely followed by rain that just buckets down. For someone who grew up in a very cool climate and isn't really a hot weather person, Kununurra's climate presented a constant challenge.

It was also the smallest town I'd ever been in, much less lived in.

In the late '80s there was very little infrastructure in place. The town had only a few shops and one very small supermarket. There was no going down the street to buy whatever you needed. A lot of things had to be ordered in specially.

But I found a way to thrive up there despite the challenges.

Kununurra was where I became more interested in health and wellbeing, and where my passion for natural therapies was fanned from a spark into a flame.

I remember discovering a little health shop early on in my search for supplies. It was a cute little shop, very old fashioned. I fell in love with it immediately, and because I was working Monday to Friday at the time I said to the owner, 'Look, if you need someone to help out on Saturday mornings, I'd love to do that'. She took me up on the offer.

KUNUNURRA =
THE VERY DEFINITION OF
'REMOTE'! – – – –

I loved those Saturday mornings! The work gave me the opportunity to interact with like-minded people, as well as an appreciation of the link between good internal health and a person's general wellness. So much so, I ended up doing further study on the topic.

Keep in mind that this was pre-internet, and I was living in an incredibly remote town. But that didn't stop me. I eventually got some information sent from a college in Queensland and threw myself into learning everything I could about giving your body the right conditions to heal itself.

When I'm really interested in something, I absolutely devour it. Well, I devoured everything they sent me.

I was also learning a lot about business in general. I moved out of my supervisory role at the hotel and over to the head office to work as an assistant to the accountant for seven of the group's properties. This gave me an excellent grounding in how businesses work from a financial point of view. I was also very fortunate that I got to keep my job when the company had to downsize for financial reasons.

I also met someone up there—Tony. And because of him, I ended up staying in Kununurra for three years. Much longer than the six months I'd intended to.

BACK TO PERTH

Eventually it was time for Tony and I to move back to a less remote location. You might laugh at me calling Perth less remote—it's the most isolated capital city in the world. But it's only one or two flights away from New Zealand instead of the three flights and many arduous hours it took from Kununurra. And Perth came with the added benefit of a temperate Mediterranean climate.

So we moved back there in 1991, and I started working for a chain of retail stores and then a computer company in South Perth. I was doing admin work, which certainly wasn't setting my world on fire. What *did* fuel my passions was visiting the local health shop near where I worked. I got to know the owner and would head over there during most of my lunch breaks. She was so open with her advice and encouraging of my interests in health and wellbeing. We'd have long chats about everything to do with natural health.

And this got me thinking, 'This is *exactly* what I want to be doing'.

Should I start my own health store? It seemed like such a logical next step. For years I'd been interested in wellness and complementary therapies, and had taken a holistic view to health for just as long. My time working in the health store in Kununurra, along with the extra study I'd done, fed the flames of that interest and I felt the time was right to explore it further.

I chatted with Roger, a friend who was a business advisor, and floated the idea with him. 'Do you think I can do this?'

Roger gave me the support and business advice I needed. He had a clear understanding of my passion, and could see that when I really wanted to do something I had the strength and tenacity to make it work.

Tony and I had just bought a house in Perth, and while he was also fully supportive we didn't have a lot of money to fund a new venture. So, it had to be done very responsibly and economically.

In the end we took a deep breath, and I quit my job and started The Health Cottage—a health and wellness store in a little suburban shopping centre in Duncraig, a suburb north of Perth.

Right up until the night before we opened, as we were busy stocking shelves and preparing to open the next morning, our view was, 'Look, if it doesn't work, it doesn't work'.

But the reality was I was never going to allow it to *not* work. I knew I had the passion, purpose and work ethic to make the venture a success.

BACKING YOURSELF

In business, Seth Godin describes something he calls The Dip:

> *At the beginning, when you first start something, it's fun. Over the next few days and weeks, the rapid learning you experience keeps you going. And then The Dip happens. The Dip is the long slog between starting and mastery ... If you can get through The Dip, if you can keep going when the system is expecting you to stop, you will achieve extraordinary results.*

When I'm mentoring people I often help them process feelings of self-doubt when in The Dip. How do I keep them moving forward at those times? I tell them:

> *You have to back yourself. If you're not backing yourself, then you don't really believe what you're trying to do is possible. And if you don't believe something's possible, what's going to get you through the hard times (i.e. The Dip)?*

Quite often they push back and ask, 'How do you know something is worth pushing through the hard times for?'

My take? It's worth it if it's something you can bring your passion and purpose to.

Experience has shown me that when you combine your passion and purpose with undying belief and a motherload of positive attention, you can achieve the most extraordinary things.

● ● ●

THE HEALTH COTTAGE

Since I didn't have money for a big fitout, I set the store up very simply. So simply, in fact, that it only took me a couple of days.

How did I know what to stock? I asked my network of trusted advisors, who at the time were the owner of the South Perth health store and my naturopath. Both were extremely supportive and provided guidance on what I needed to have in the store.

As luck would have it, the store was located directly opposite the supermarket. It was a great spot for visibility and curiosity as people would come out of the supermarket, see the store, and wander over for a look.

I must have done something right with those early 'curious' customers because word began to spread, and my sales and clientele began to grow quite steadily. I developed a great connection with my customers and began to intuitively know what people were *really* looking for when they came to see me. Sometimes it was advice on boosting their immune system naturally. Sometimes it was a treatment for their eczema. But a lot of the time, it was just to be heard.

My first foray into small business - owner of the Health Cottage

It became evident how lonely people are, and how so many of them don't have anyone they feel they can confide in. I could provide this support, and it was through listening to others and giving them the opportunity to talk that helped me understand how many health concerns can be driven as much by our emotions as our mental and physical wellbeing.

I ended up having a private room in the store, which was always stocked with tissues. I loved how people could walk into my store and feel it was a safe space to share whatever was most ailing their minds or bodies at the time.

The Health Cottage was a lovely and gentle introduction into the world of small business. I opened it in 1994, so extended trading hours and Sunday trading weren't a thing. I had Sundays off, and on Saturdays I'd close up around three in the afternoon. Weekdays were usual trading days, and we didn't close until 5.30-6.00pm. This still gave me plenty of time to pursue more study and look after myself from a fitness point of view. I was going to the gym three times a week, and I'd often walk to work if the weather permitted.

I'd also started working with aromatherapy and essential oils, and my customers were getting great results from blends I created for them. It was around this time that I learned about an Aroma Tour to Provence in the south of France. Participants would get the chance to meet world-renowned aromatherapy leaders and be educated by them via two weeks of intensive learning.

I was torn. The Health Cottage had only been going for 18 months and getting to France and spending two weeks there was a significant financial investment. There was also the fact that I'd have to pay someone to run the shop while I was away.

But my intuition, which I've relied on heavily throughout my life, told me I just had to get myself there. And my intuition was right.

TUNING IN TO YOUR INTUITION

It's often hard to discern between intuition and impetuousness. A lot of people wonder if you don't want to do something straight away, then do you really want to do it at all? I come at it from a different direction. I actively ask for affirmation that something is the right thing to do. Over the years I've realised I get that affirmation via a feeling of 'connectedness' when I know it's the right thing. Sometimes I can even see how things are going to play out.

In the case of the Provence tour, I didn't have any choice but to wait for affirmation. I couldn't go to their website, find out all the information and impetuously sign up for the tour with money I didn't have. I had to send away for information and wait for the tour information booklet to arrive via the post.

And when it did, the booklet specified participants would be shown a lavender distillation. I'd always had an association with France and dreamt of going to Paris. But it was that specific, and very non-generic term 'lavender distillation' that sealed the deal for me. Ever since I became interested in aromatherapy I'd had a desire to experience a lavender distillation.

I thought, 'That's it. I'm going to do this'.

Since I didn't have the money to pay for the trip, I worked hard and ran aromatherapy workshops.

I just had to make it happen. And I did.

PROVENCE

I completely fell in love with Provence—the air, the aromas, the food, the light. It's hard to describe, but I immediately understood why all the impressionist artists went there to paint. My senses instantly came alive on arrival, and the clarity of thought I experienced there was stunning.

For the entire two weeks of the tour my senses were overloaded as I got to smell and enjoy some of the most exquisite essential oils I'd ever worked with. I learned so much from the amazing educators, and had my eyes opened wide regarding the quality of essential oils available.

It was on that trip that the very first seeds of Sodashi were planted.

I remember asking the educators, 'Is anyone doing anything with essential oils and skin care?' And the answer was, 'Not really'. While some people were dabbling, no-one was using essential oils as the active ingredient.

In fact, I was in France with Robbi and Jim (the tour organisers) while writing this book, and Robbi recalls the conversation very clearly.

'You told Jim and I on that very first trip that you were going home to make skin care products with essential oils. You were very determined'.

Well, yes. I was. And when I arrived back home, it became my new project.

Why skin care? The main reason was I had sensitive skin and hadn't been able to find a product that didn't make my skin react but was also results-driven and effective.

So right from the beginning I had a very good test case for product development—me. I decided to go with all-natural ingredients because I'd been thinking for some time about how

Robbi and me in the beautiful lavender fields of Provence

our skin is our largest organ, and if you aren't willing to put something *into* your body you probably shouldn't be putting it *on* your skin.

Sue, one of the ladies I met in Provence, had a formula for a very basic cream made with clean ingredients, and she showed me how she formulated that cream. Another aromatherapist on our course, Ron, had started doing courses on regenerative skin care using plant oils and essential oils. I attended his workshops and enjoyed his experimental approach, and decided I would take that approach too.

WHEN THE STUDENT IS READY, THE TEACHER APPEARS

Robbi, Jim and their Provence aromatherapy tour presented themselves at exactly the right time in my life—a point where I had enough time and knowledge to both apply the teachings and take them one step further.

And it's worth noting the role Ron played in supporting me with the information I needed to take it one step further. When I was back in Perth I attended some of his courses on creating natural skin care. Although I didn't use many of his recommended ingredients, what I got from his courses was the confidence to play, experiment and push boundaries.

And that's what I did with Sodashi. I pushed boundaries, combining plant oils and essential oils in my own creative ways while constantly researching and developing.

I always tell people that when you want to do something, find someone you can learn the basic skills from. But don't just learn the way someone else does it and copy them. Ideally, find someone you can learn from while still being able to develop and implement your own unique creativity.

If you're learning from people you're aligned to, they'll give you the confidence and knowledge to put your own stamp on things. And I felt aligned to everyone I learned from in those early days of aromatherapy and skin care.

—— • ● • ——

'LAURA'S FACE CREAM'

By early 1996 I had formulated my first face moisturiser and started using it on my skin. Within a week I could see the effects.

The success markers I set for myself were:

- For my skin not to react to the cream. (My skin reacted to so many other skin care products I tried.)

- To observe beneficial results. (I won't keep using a product if my skin isn't responding positively and the results aren't clearly visible.)

Not only did my skin not react, my complexion completely changed. The integrity of my skin changed as well, and I had a glow. So much so, customers at The Health Cottage started commenting on it and asking me what I was using.

When I said it was a cream I was making for myself, they asked if I had any they could purchase. As it happened, I did. (There's a limit to how small a batch you can make at any one time, so I always had a few extra pots on hand.) Whenever someone asked for some cream I'd go out the back to my workroom, personalise the base cream for them using essential oils most suited to their skin type, stick a label on the pot that said something like 'Laura's Face Cream' and voila.

Humble beginnings indeed.

It soon got to the point where I was making a new batch of ten or so pots on a weekend, and they'd all be gone the following week. So I decided it was time to make bigger batches—50 pots at a time.

That first batch of 50 pots lasted around four weeks. But the next batch lasted only two weeks, and then I was moving through 50 pots a week. At this point my now partner Ken had to go out for breakfast in the mornings because he'd come into the kitchen and I'd be telling him, 'Sorry, you can't do anything in here. I've sterilised the kitchen so I can make a new batch of cream'.

For all the success of the cream, at this early stage it was still just a fun project rather than a serious business enterprise. I didn't think much of it until one day in 1997 when someone drove all the way from Rockingham to my shop in Duncraig—a 150km round trip—to buy a cream for herself. All on the strength of a verbal recommendation from a friend.

Remember, this was 1997. Google was still a year away, and Mark Zuckerberg was only 13 years old. So the only way word-of-mouth could work was by people actually talking to each other.

I was stunned that my cream had been recommended so strongly. And inside I was feeling all sorts of excitement that someone was willing to drive all that way to buy a pot. It was a real turning point.

BE SO GOOD PEOPLE CAN'T HELP BUT TALK ABOUT YOU

I remember speaking with a marketing guru in Perth in the early 2000s who said, *'Do what you do so well that people can't help but talk about you'*.

Social media and the online world had very little influence on business growth back in 1997. You *had* to offer a great product or service, and you *really had* to do what you did so well that people would tell others about it.

Even with the explosion of social media, I've always sought to align Sodashi with people who talk about the brand because they truly believe in it. I want them to post about it because they genuinely love the products and achieve fabulous results, not because the company is paying them a huge amount of money. Otherwise it just becomes paid advertising through another portal.

The marketing basics I believe will never let you down are:

- Having a great product.
- Treating your customers well and listening to what they say. (Happy customers are your best sales force.)
- Providing authentic and valuable education.

So while we've certainly embraced social media today, and set up some wise and clever collaborations,

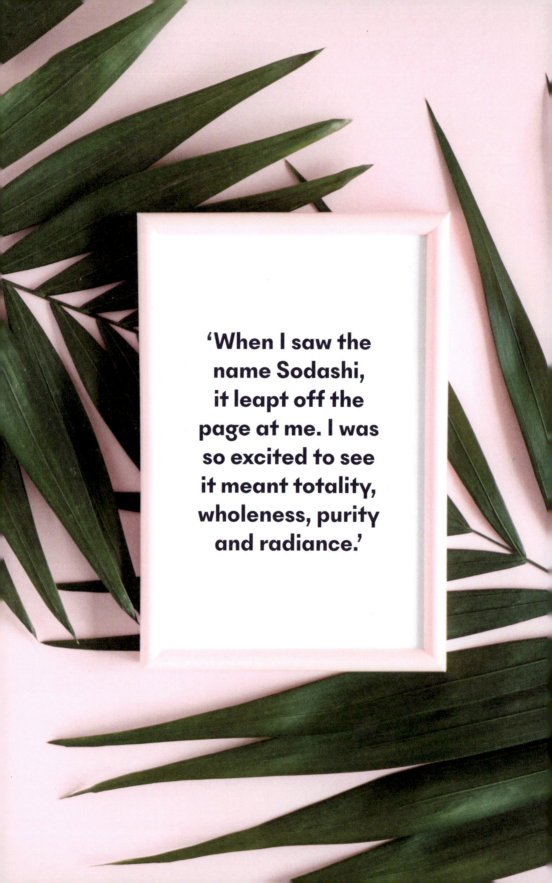

'When I saw the name Sodashi, it leapt off the page at me. I was so excited to see it meant totality, wholeness, purity and radiance.'

that side of our brand's marketing efforts simply wouldn't work without the foundation of great products and great customer service.

And I can confidently say it's this focus that has allowed us to grow consistently year after year through our entire history (bar the Global Financial Crisis (GFC) years, where we held steady).

───────── ● ● ● ─────────

SODASHI

When 50 pots of cream were heading out the door of The Health Cottage each week, Ken suggested creating a professional name and label for the moisturiser rather than labelling each pot individually based on whoever was buying it.

So I started going through the words in a Sanskrit dictionary. I wanted a Sanskrit name because I'd come to know and love Ayurveda, a very ancient Indian health care system. My fascination with Ayurveda led to a fascination with India in general, and I was attracted to the Sanskrit language because I liked how it sounded—soft and kind.

When I saw the name Sodashi, it leapt off the page at me. I was so excited to see it meant totality, wholeness, purity and radiance—exactly what I wanted Sodashi to be, and exactly what I wanted the products to do for the skin.

Around the same time, my customers started putting pressure on me to expand the range.

'Can you create a cleanser?'

'We need something to put around our eyes.'

So I did some more courses, and a lot of research on ingredients. I experimented widely, and had great fun trying different formulations to see what worked for different purposes and what didn't. (Formulating is still one of the great delights of my life.)

Before long I had two separate skin care ranges to address different skin concerns, each with a cleanser, concentrate, mist, moisturiser, night cream and skin boost.

All while I was still running The Health Cottage.

Someone once asked if it ever got unwieldy juggling the running of the store and the research and experimentation needed to expand the Sodashi product range. And I can honestly say it never did. I was consumed with passion and felt like I had endless energy.

But by 1998 I was approaching five years in retail, and the more my passion for aromatherapy and skin care fired up the more my passion for retail started to wane.

I knew at some stage I'd end up selling the store to go full-time with Sodashi. But when would be the right time to make the jump?

I know this is a question every founder faces at one time or another. And I don't think there are any hard and fast rules for this situation. So many things factor into the decision—your family situation, whether income from another source can pay your bills while you establish your startup venture, and your own tolerance for risk and stress.

And of course, you can only make your decision based on the information you have at the time. Here's the information I was working with:

- I didn't want to borrow lots of money to fund Sodashi. So I knew I'd be bootstrapping–drawing little or no income in the early days so I could put all the profits back into the business.

- I knew I was a bit ahead of the curve with my products. In the late '90s, natural skin care wasn't a 'thing'. Yes, I'd converted the customers at The Health Cottage very quickly. But they knew me and trusted me. Selling the idea of natural skin care to a wider market would require a whole new model of education.

- I didn't want to go from being relatively comfortable financially to being completely strung out. While I knew the possibilities would be endless once I could focus all my energies on Sodashi, I also knew what an energy sapper financial strain can be.

Essentially, I knew it would be hard bootstrapping *and* having to educate a market, but I didn't want the stress of a big loan to service. That determined the path I took.

Today I happily share with those I mentor or anyone starting a business that they'll probably need more money than they project at the start. I certainly underestimated the amount of cash we'd need.

Would I have done things differently in hindsight? Probably. But none of us are time travellers, so hindsight never gets to feature in our decision making.

Something that made transitioning out of The Health Cottage more realistic was securing the contract to provide the base cream for a company setting up environmentally friendly cleaning and personal care products. After purchasing a moisturiser from me, they asked if I could make a basic body lotion. I could, and we started supplying them with 60kg of cream a month.

As for putting The Health Cottage up for sale, I didn't even get the chance to advertise.

I've always been amazed what can happen when I focus my energies on a particular outcome. By now I was ready to sell the business because I had my next progression all lined up. I was chatting with a customer, telling her how Sodashi was getting busier and I'd have to consider selling The Health Cottage soon. She said to let her know when I was ready because she'd be interested.

I did, and she bought it.

So that was that.

I transitioned out of The Health Cottage in December 1998 and got ready to move on to the next stage of my business life.

YOUR STARTUP IDEA

So you have the seed of an idea, and you're trying to figure out if it's worth pursuing or not.

Here are ten questions from my professional experience I'd like to share with you. Answering these questions will offer some clarity about your idea and give you an idea of whether it's a good idea and whether you're the right person to bring it to life.

1. WHAT is the idea, product or service?

2. What's the WHY behind your idea/product/service? Do you have a personal reason for wanting to do this?

3. WHO will you sell it to? Who is your market? Who is your customer? Go into detail here—who is the ideal person? What's their personality and worldview? What's important to them? Where do they work? Where do they live? What does their life look like? Is there a gap in the market?

4. HOW will you sell your idea/product/service? Can you access the person you've identified in Question 3? Where do they hang out? What do you need to reach them? A website? An app? A network of contacts? A social media presence?

5. WHAT budget do you need to create the infrastructure that will help you sell your idea/product/service?

6. WHERE is the market? Is it local? National? Global? Where do you want to start?

7. If your idea is a product, do you need a creator, developer or manufacturer? WHAT are the costs associated with creating that product?

8. HOW will you finance your startup? Do you need one or more investors?

9. WOULD you benefit from a business coach or mentor?

10. At WHAT stage does your startup business need to start supporting you financially?

LEARNING TO EXPECT THE UNEXPECTED

I don't know too many people who get to transition from one business to another by taking a holiday, but I highly recommend it.

After handing The Health Cottage over to the new owner in early 1999, I headed to New Zealand with Ken and his kids. Because I hadn't properly started Sodashi at this stage, I didn't need to talk to anyone or keep tabs on anything at home. I could hit the off button, be very 'in the moment' and really enjoy the beauty of it all. It was a great time.

Once back in Perth, my intention was to gently cruise through the first third of the year to ensure my energy levels were fully topped up and then, come April, be 'all systems go' with Sodashi. And the plan went along swimmingly right up to March when I got a call to say my father was in hospital.

He and my mother separated when I was very young, and he hadn't been a big part of my life for many years. But he was living in Western Australia, so I did see him on occasion.

When I saw him in hospital he was resting easily, but things escalated quickly from there. The next call I got was to say he was in ICU on life support. By the time I arrived at the hospital all his organs were shutting down. Within eight hours I was forced to make the decision to turn off the machines keeping him alive.

It was a surreal and harrowing time.

My brother flew over from New Zealand for the funeral, but had to leave soon after. While he did come back and help me sort out and sell Dad's property, for practical reasons the job of executing Dad's will and administering his estate fell to me.

So, here I was, dealing with the emotional aftermath of my father's death, managing all the paperwork of an estate that had many moving parts and wasn't in any kind of order, and about to throw myself full-time into a new business.

It was one of those if-you-don't-laugh-you'll-cry situations. In the end, I did both.

I was totally unprepared for the time and emotional energy it took to process my father's sudden death. But I had to get moving.

How did I do it? Well, I just did it.

THE IMPORTANCE OF RESILIENCE

It's almost fitting that the 'full-time with Sodashi' journey started this way because it was an early lesson:

It doesn't matter how neatly you set things up in business, sometimes life will just happen.

And when it *does* happen, you just have to deal with it.

It's important to remember that while you can't control how life comes at you, you *can* control how you come at life (and business).

I've already spoken about resilience being one of the major things I learned from my mother while growing up. That resilience has meant that while my reaction to things is often something like 'Shit, are you kidding me?' accompanied by a bit of venting, I don't dwell. (Because what's the point?)

Anne was my first hire. Today she is a dear friend and frequent travel partner of mine

But I *do* like to have a sounding board, and certainly seek the company of the wise on these occasions. From there I can generally take the situation, turn it around in my head so I can see it clearly, formulate a path forward that I think is best, and get my feet on that path as quickly as is possible and practical.

The reason I can do this so effectively is my reserves of resilience are continually being replenished by strong self-care practices. I believe it's one of my greatest 'secret weapons' in business, and why I've dedicated a whole section of the book to that topic.

● ● ●

THE FIRST HIRE

Beyond my hard-earned reserves of resilience, something that helped me move forward with Sodashi while dealing with my father's death and the administration of his estate was making my first hire.

Anne, who I met through The Health Cottage, offered her services when I went full-time with Sodashi and officially started with me in April 1999. At the time I didn't know what my needs would be in terms of staff. But it quickly became clear what a huge risk it was for me to be the only person who could make the Sodashi products.

Initially Anne was someone I could train to manufacture the products. But she became so much more than that. Together we took care of everything: answering the phone, taking orders, talking with clients, customer service, dispatch, documentation, the lot. She was my right hand and confidante.

She was also incredibly invested in the business. One night in our first year we worked until 2.30am to get a big order out. Nothing was ever too much trouble for her. When you're in the early stages of a startup you need people around you who are willing to pitch in and just get the job done. You also need someone you can trust to tell you things straight, but with respect. Anne ticked all those boxes and more.

I loved being able to give her a job she could do flexibly around her three kids. And she loved being able to give me the flexibility of working longer hours when I needed extra help.

She went on to be our manufacturing manager and work for me for 18 years. She's also one of my closest and dearest friends to this day.

Once my father's estate was taken care of, I could finally turn all my attention and energy to Sodashi. It was an exciting time.

My main feeling at the start of it all? A combination of determination and curiosity.

Not sure where I was going with the venture, I was looking forward to seeing how things played out. I was determined it would go somewhere. But I got the feeling those close to me thought it was another one of 'Megan's harebrained schemes'.

BEING TAKEN SERIOUSLY

In the early days of Sodashi, my family and friends struggled to see the venture as more than a hobby. Even my accountant didn't take it seriously. (If he did, we'd have set the business up quite differently at the start and saved some pain further down the track.)

When I look back, I can see that the enthusiasm and energy I brought to the venture made it easy for people to view it as little more than a passion project. I was also so caught up in doing everything in the business that I never really took the time to communicate where I was at, what I was doing, and where I wanted to go.

Business life is easier when those close to you are on the same page.

If I'd sat down with my loved ones and shared my vision for the business more openly (instead of expecting them to be mind-readers), I wouldn't have had to wait a couple of years for them to take the business seriously and give me the level of support I craved.

THE PERILS OF BEING A PIONEER

In that first year, manufacturing the base creams for the contracts we had kept Anne and me busy. We also started supplying to a couple of local Perth beauty salons, which was a good start because at that point I felt they'd be our main market.

But I ran into the same problem most pioneers face: we were way ahead of our time.

'All-natural' wasn't a thing in 1999. So instead of simply being able to *sell* the Sodashi products on their merits, I had to spend a huge amount of time *educating* the market about why all-natural was important when it came to skin care, and how our unique formulations made our products incredibly effective.

Initially I didn't see the challenge because I was fuelled with such passion, purpose and determination to share something with the world that I knew was amazing. I'd seen the transformation in both my own skin and the skin of people close to me who used it, so I knew we were on to a good thing.

While doubts may have flashed through my head at times, I never wanted to entertain them because I knew if I did it would be my undoing.

Being ahead of your time and having to educate the market (especially when you're bootstrapping your business) takes a great deal of energy. Much more than the average startup requires.

You must also be quite single-minded, and a bit pigheaded. It's not because you don't *want* to listen to anyone else. It's more because you *must* have absolute self-belief. And when you're in that zone, you can't afford the distraction of the naysayers.

You need to conserve your energy for all the barriers you have to push through.

In my case, the barriers were:

- *How can natural possibly work?*
- *What do you mean this will do more for me than my clinically-proven, chemically made face cream?*
- *What do you mean your products are made with love, intention and pure energy?*

It's funny. Back in the early days of Sodashi I gave each staff member the chance to learn and practise Transcendental Meditation. Today it's seen as a hallmark of how progressive and dialled in we are as a company. But go back 15 years and you'll see we stopped telling people we did that because they just didn't get it.

It's the same with *holistic, energy* and *intention*. People use these words every day now. But in our early years people found it all 'a bit hippie trippy'. So we'd get back in our little bubble and keep pushing on and pushing through all the barriers by virtue of self-belief and pigheadedness.

And that's where I was at when someone approached me to be the master distributor for Sodashi. Which goes a little way towards explaining why I jumped on board with them so quickly— *too* quickly, as it turned out. I felt securing that relationship would allow Anne and me to focus on manufacturing while someone else took the responsibility of securing new clients and delivering the product. At the time, a master distributor felt like the missing piece in the Sodashi puzzle.

But in the end, the relationship didn't serve me or Sodashi very well. If I had my time again I'd have been less desperate to hand over such a crucial part of my business, no matter how much it seemed the answer to all my prayers. And I'd have done it with a bit more due diligence by speaking to other brands they were distributing.

Since they were also a new business, I saw it as an opportunity to grow together. But really what I needed was a level of expertise beyond my own which they simply didn't have.

It took me a year to extract Sodashi from that relationship, which created a lot of stress during a time that was already stressful.

'Given my lack of a 'big failure' story, you may be thinking, 'Maybe she was just really risk averse."

THE 'ALL IS LOST' MOMENT IS NOT COMPULSORY

When you're writing a book like this one, your editor might say:

Every good startup story, especially one that's been going for 19 years, will have an 'all is lost' moment. At some point in the narrative, something earth-shattering will happen that causes the founder to think, 'This is it, the dream is over'. But then the founder will rally, find the resilience and resources to surmount the insurmountable challenge. And once they've met that challenge, all future challenges will pale into insignificance.

Spoiler alert: I've never had one of those moments. I don't have a big, inspiring 'back from the brink of failure' story to share.

The closest I've been is when I discovered the master distributor wasn't paying us the money they were meant to. I felt so frustrated and powerless I broke down sobbing on the floor of my bathroom.

But while that was a hard time, and while there are things I'd do differently today, it wasn't an insurmountable challenge. Just an incredibly frustrating and distracting one.

Given my lack of a 'big failure' story, you may be thinking, 'Maybe she was just really risk averse', or, 'She never thought big enough', or 'She wasn't in a hurry, so she didn't have to go fast and break things'. There is truth to those statements, but I think the real reason is that small mistakes tend to be revealed to me before they become big mistakes.

And I make sure I tune in to them because small mistakes are much easier to recover from or pivot around.

Once again, I thank my self-care practices for this. I'll talk more about the role they play in helping you see situations for what they are later in this book.

GOING INTERNATIONAL

There was one blessing that came out of the whole master distributor debacle. They connected me with two ladies who'd been an essential part of a Beauty College in Queensland and then went on to set up other businesses. One ended up being a distributor for Sodashi in Queensland, while the other had her own practice in Sydney and was using Sodashi products.

It was amazing to have their support and backing at the time. They showed me the power of finding your tribe and having people around you who spoke the same language.

They were also on hand to help me at the one and only trade show Sodashi ever exhibited at. This trade show was significant because it's where I connected with Chrissy, who was the Spa Director of the Sheraton in Bangkok at the time. The fact Sodashi was trailblazing natural skin care really captured her attention. Like me, she was a bit ahead of her time in seeing that spas, as places of wellness and wellbeing, should be using all-natural products wherever possible.

This kicked off Sodashi's initial foray into the international spa market.

We started working with Chrissy at the end of 2001, with the aim of launching Sodashi into Sheraton Bangkok in October 2002.

It was a crazy time as we were trying to figure it all out as we went along.

It took many phone calls and a lot of back and forth to get things started. Chrissy and I met up a few times, and then I travelled to Bangkok several times over the following year to set things up.

When you're the first person to do something, there's no blueprint. You have to make things up as you go along. There were no steps I could follow for exporting an Australian natural product into Thailand, much less navigating all the paperwork and red tape around packaging and ingredients to be met, and the regulations for importing our products. (Although being an all-natural product made that easier.)

Making the learning curve even steeper was having to learn the difference between beauty therapy treatments (which is what we'd been developing for the Sodashi products) and spa treatments. Beauty therapy treatments are more functional—the client is looking for a *specific result*. But spa treatments, while still results-focused, are *all about the experience*. They should be a beautiful blend of effectiveness and relaxation, something that ultimately supports the customer's wellbeing.

At the time Thailand was leading the way with their approach to spa treatments, and it was fascinating to be brought into that world. Many of my trips to Bangkok were spent visiting spas and getting an understanding of how our products fit into their model. From there I'd go home to develop the treatments, and then go back to Bangkok to train their therapists in the use of our products.

From the very beginning it's been important to me that our spa therapists are exceptional ambassadors for the Sodashi brand. Training international, non-English speaking therapists in the use of our products for Sheraton Bangkok involved a steep learning curve. But it also allowed us to push into other non-English speaking markets more quickly and smoothly.

FAKE IT TILL YOU MAKE IT

If Instagram existed back then, and I was sharing what was going on in the business on that platform, you'd be forgiven for thinking we were #killingit. On the surface it looked very glamorous and lucrative—travelling to Bangkok, working with the spa director at this beautiful hotel, and having a massive launch for our brand in that hotel.

But in reality we were investing a huge amount of time and money in blazing the all-natural trail and building everything—relationships, treatment protocols, training protocols—from scratch.

While I did take on a small loan from my friend Julie after we'd been in business for around six months (which Julie eventually converted into shares to become our first shareholder), we were still bootstrapping the business. This meant the growth and development of Sodashi was driven by the income we were making from our base cream contracts, sales into local Perth beauty salons, and Ken's and my personal savings and credit cards that were now maxed out.

Looking back, I can see Sodashi really needed around $250,000 in capital at the start. But we only had $120,000, so we were undercapitalised from the beginning. It took around six years to make Sodashi an international brand, and it needed an investment from Ken and me of something close to a million dollars.

I didn't draw a wage from the business until 2003, and even then it was a pretty meagre one. For many years everyone else in the business was being paid more than I was.

But I certainly couldn't share any of that back then.

At the time of writing this book, vulnerability and authenticity are all the rage. Founders are sharing the realities of their journey while running around in jeans and sneakers. Lucky them, I say. It's exactly how it should be.

But in 2002 it was all about faking it until you made it. People, especially major international spa brands taking a chance on a pioneering Australian all-natural product, had to see you were successful. Otherwise you were just too big a risk.

So yes, everything looked shiny from the outside. The Sheraton made a big deal about the launch of Sodashi into their spa, and they had a huge event for all the local media the night before. Again, if Instagram had existed back then that's all you would have seen.

What you wouldn't have known is that I ate something the night before that gave me terrible food poisoning. The two Sodashi staff who came to support the event found me hunched on my bathroom floor. Even after their dash to the local pharmacy for something to help peel me off the bathroom floor, I still spent most of the launch rushing off to the bathroom wracked by the horrendous pain that comes with food poisoning.

Looking back, I'm bemused at what an apt metaphor that experience was for my life at the time.

GROWTH

The spa at Sheraton Bangkok was quite large, and run very efficiently. Once Sodashi had launched into that spa, I travelled regularly to Bangkok to help support them and their staff. It was a great education for me being there on the ground, talking directly with the spa director. I quickly learned what we needed to change and improve.

Shortly after our launch at Sheraton Bankgok, we attracted the attention of JW Marriott in Bangkok and started working with them as well.

Around this time I was delighted to meet Karina Stewart who, along with her husband John, are visionaries in the spa industry, especially around health and wellbeing. I was always inspired by our chats, so whenever I was in Bangkok I'd try to meet up and chat.

Karina is one of the founding partners of Kamalaya in Koh Samui, Thailand. It would be many years until Sodashi products made their way into their beautiful resort, but I adored having someone so aligned with my values and professional interests to talk to and use as a sounding board.

It was also around this time that we went online for the first time.

A website is the first thing most people would start with today, because without one people won't think you're serious or a real business.

Back then, it was less of a priority but for Sodashi, it was a game changer.

Not only was the website a beautiful online brochure for us, it also had an online shop. This meant travellers going to beautiful overseas spas and experiencing our products could continue buying them when they returned home.

In late 2002, Six Senses, who had spas in Thailand and the Maldives, got in touch with us and wanted to co-brand a product with them. This was one of my greatest learning experiences, and one of the greatest things for the business.

Co-branding with a brand of spas is much different to placing your products in a spa (which is what we'd been doing up to this point). When you co-brand, you're endorsing their brand and they're endorsing yours. So you really need to make sure it's the right partnership.

Six Senses, headed by Sonu and Eva Shivdasani at the time, believed in the environment, sustainability, organic and natural. It made perfect sense for us to align with them. Additionally, their brand was highly regarded in the spa industry, and co-branding with them gave us more recognition and credibility while also boosting the Sodashi profile internationally.

'We were very agile and could roll with the punches as they came. This meant we could learn from mistakes very quickly.'

Practically speaking, I didn't realise that because co-branding meant new packaging (i.e. different artwork) it would also mean re-registering all the products for import into Thailand.

There were also a few random curveballs to deal with. Six Senses had properties in the Maldives, and on one occasion we shipped products there when the port had gone on strike. The products didn't get clearance, and sat on the wharf in extreme heat for a couple of months. When the products were finally cleared, each package had to be opened and checked because they'd been subjected to intense heat. Products we couldn't be sure weren't damaged were destroyed. We lost a lot of product that day.

If there was ever a time in Sodashi's development where we felt a little behind the eight ball and like we were winging it a bit, it was co-branding with Six Senses.

But we were very agile and could roll with the punches as they came. This meant we could learn from mistakes very quickly. Thankfully none of the mistakes we made were huge, business-killing ones.

We successfully launched into Six Senses in Thailand with our co-branded product in mid-2003, and shortly after in to the Maldives.

In Australia, we were invited to tender for the Voyager group of hotels. This was our first ever tender, and we were successful. It involved several trips to Australia's east coast to meet with the Voyager spa director before launching first at their Cradle Mountain Spa, and then into Queensland. This helped establish us as a spa brand in Australia.

In 2004 we took on our first American distributor. But the US was a tough market to crack. The desire for all-natural skin care just wasn't there, and we had to do a huge amount of education to get the meagre penetration we achieved.

Later that year I took on my second investor. As I mentioned earlier, at this point Sodashi was almost completely bootstrapped (except for the small converted loan from Julie). But I met someone who was very interested in what we were doing and how we were doing it. There was some due diligence and investigation involved in her coming on board, and it provided an interesting opportunity to reflect and see the business through outside eyes.

We put that funding to good use. In 2001 we'd moved from our original converted garage premises to a similar setup in South Perth where our offices and manufacturing were in different premises. And we'd long outgrown both.

Taking on an investor meant we could move from South Perth to North Fremantle and have our office and manufacturing in one place. We're still at those North Fremantle premises today.

In 2005 we entered the Middle East when Six Senses opened a spa in Dubai, and later expanded in to Qatar.

The years 2006-2008 saw us expand into Europe and Ireland. For both territories we found distributors who were passionate about the brand and spa industry. They weren't experienced distributors, but we supported each other as the brand distribution grew.

Sodashi launched in Paris into the Four Seasons Hotel George V in 2008 before being rolled out in other Four Seasons Hotels, and then expanded into five more countries across Europe. We also started exporting into Russia, and while it was good at a time where most of the Western world was feeling the effects of the GFC, after a few years it became challenging. Russia is a hard country to work with.

In late 2008 and early 2009 we began talks with Aman Resorts. This was hugely exciting and validating, as Aman was still owned by Adrian Zecha—a renowned visionary of the hotel and spa industry. Sodashi went on to develop a 30-product signature line for Aman Resorts, which was released into 20 of their spas globally and used throughout the time Adrian owned the resorts.

The transition from 2009 to 2010 brought with it a change in shareholders. The investor who joined me in 2004 had a different vision for the company, and she wanted to take the business in a different direction. In the end, we parted ways.

This was a really challenging time for me. But the new shareholders, along with a new board member, brought good, solid expertise to the table and really helped Sodashi take the next step.

WORKING WITH SHAREHOLDERS

If you're a founder looking to take on investors (which means having to report to shareholders), chances are you've heard people talk about the pros and cons of this scenario, with the cons mostly being around the potential loss of control.

I'll admit I found this challenging when I first took on investments for the business. I was used to making the decisions and found it difficult having to report to other people and run certain decisions by co-directors and company management first.

My great friend Julie was Sodashi's first investor after converting a small loan she made to me in the early days into shares

Here are my tips for deciding whether it's the right time to take on investors and/or shareholders:

- Do they have experience working with founders of startups? It's important that prospective shareholders know how to get the best out of you as a founder.

- Find investors (and therefore shareholders) you can respect and will treat you with respect.

- As a founder you never want to lose your passion, purpose or 'why?', so consider the timing carefully to preserve these vital things.

Here are my tips for working well with your shareholders:

- Since you're going to be held accountable, quickly align with your shareholders' expectations so you can be dynamic and experimental.

- Ensure you have a good line of communication.

- Use their feedback positively. If you don't agree, be prepared to have robust and progressive conversations.

When you have people asking hard questions about your operations, it forces you to assess situations more critically. When you make promises, you need to either deliver on them or explain clearly why you can't.

While some of my greatest challenges have come from my shareholders, so too have some of my greatest learnings.

WHEN THE PERSONAL AND PROFESSIONAL COLLIDE

In 2009 we appointed our first general manager (GM). And, of course, we did it the startup way—by appointing someone who came on board early and had grown with the company.

Jessica first started with us as a receptionist, and then became one of our amazing educators who travelled overseas and trained the spa staff in the use of our products. She helped trailblaze Sodashi into the global arena and was a very passionate ambassador of the brand.

She also found a way to convince me she could take her job to Melbourne for a couple of years. But I was thrilled when she decided to return to Perth. I really enjoyed making her GM in 2009, as it felt like she was an extension of me.

Jessica managed the operational side of the business. That gave me time to drive the business creatively, work with the other directors on business growth and development and focus on founder activities—building relationships, media events, etc.

This meant I was travelling a lot between 2009 and 2011. I was always out meeting new clients, cementing existing relationships, building new relationships, and expanding into new markets.

Even though it looked like the world was coming out the other side of the GFC, we spent 2010 and 2011 managing our growth with caution. During 2011 we expanded further into the Middle East by appointing a distributor on the ground.

It was also the start of a personally challenging time for me because at the end of 2011 I separated from Ken.

I'd love to say I managed to keep the personal turmoil out of my professional life. But few people have the ability to compartmentalise, and I'm definitely not one of them. The end of any relationship, romantic or otherwise, that's spanned 16 years is going to rock your world. Looking back, I can see I just went into survival mode, doing the best I could to protect both myself and the business.

To complicate things further, I met and started seeing someone new just seven months after officially separating from Ken. Starting a new relationship when you've got a business is really hard. What gets your attention? In my case, the new relationship was getting a lot of attention.

Working in Sodashi's favour was the fact that Jessica had been with us for 12 years—two years as GM. And Sodashi's manufacturing manager, Anne, had been with us for 14 years.

Looking back, I realise this is what gave me the confidence and freedom to invest so fully in my new relationship. It also gave me the confidence to do what I did next.

Paul lived in Sydney with his four children. Towards the end of 2012 I got to thinking, 'We can keep doing this long-distance thing, or I can relocate'.

I broached the idea with Jessica, who was supportive, and we announced it to the rest of the team in early January 2013.

This is where I got a lesson in communication. I expected a lot of people, especially those who'd been working with Sodashi for years, to do a fair amount of reading between the lines. I expected the reaction to be something like, 'Oh, yeah. We saw this coming'.

Instead, a couple of team members were furious. They couldn't understand how their founder could relocate to a different city from where the business was based—especially when that city was a four to five hour flight away.

'I had an idea of the kind of leader I wanted to be. I wanted to lead with my heart, focus on the greater good, and not ask others to do anything I wouldn't do myself.'

But I was determined to make it work.

I moved to Sydney in February 2013, and it was quite a shock. As I write this book and reflect on that time, I recall the difficulties I faced moving to a new city. Yes, I was with Paul. But I hadn't just left my company behind back in Perth. I'd left behind my Sodashi family.

So I now faced an entirely different day. Instead of heading into an office and seeing my Sodashi family every day, I was working from home by myself. I also didn't have a network of friends to call on like those I left behind in Perth, so I felt very isolated and lonely. It took a good two years to find my feet, build my networks, and become familiar enough with my new city to feel at home.

It was also difficult for my team in Perth. Because I felt so isolated I was calling them several times a day to feel connected and be part of things. It took me a while to realise they needed to be left alone to get on with their work, and I needed to find a way of coping.

AS A FOUNDER, YOU ARE ALSO A LEADER

My transition from developing/creating products to setting up a company and making it all real was quite a challenge for me. I had no real idea about leadership, nor did I have strong management skills.

But I had an idea of the kind of leader I wanted to be. I wanted to lead with my heart, focus on the greater good, and not ask others to do anything I wouldn't do myself.

Passion wasn't something I lacked, which meant I found it very challenging when others didn't share that passion. It took someone to point out that if my employees had just 20% of the passion I had, I was doing well. (As it turned out, many of them were way above that 20% mark.)

In the early years of my business I was so busy doing that I didn't invest enough time in some relationships. When people moved on from Sodashi, it seemed to observers that I moved on from them too quickly. Looking back, I can see I was using busyness to avoid the question of why they left and what I, as leader of the company, could learn from their exit.

That's when I started to work on balancing conviction with connection. I started working on my emotional intelligence (something I do to this day), empathy and flexibility.

That flexibility made me more open to the realities of others and their perspectives. As I practised it more and more, I started making better decisions and coming at things with more clarity.

I won't pretend I'm a perfect leader today. Who is? But I've learned so much over the years about the balance needed to do the job well. And I'm committed to continuing my education in that arena in the years to come.

LETTING GO OF THE REINS

In 2014 Jessica resigned as GM to move back to Melbourne.

This brought a new GM to the team, Donna; someone who was very different to Jessica, who, as I've mentioned, felt like an extension of me. And while the shift in personalities and strengths was quite challenging, I could see how the systems and processes Donna began implementing would benefit the business.

Their contrasting styles showed me how important it is to strike a balance. You need to find a way to nurture and care for your team while also nurturing and caring for your business. A profitable business is best able to support its people. But you need to treat your people well for the business to be profitable.

I'm not sure I was ready for the next three years. But the timing was right.

While Sodashi was my baby and I didn't really want to cut the apron strings, I needed to so it could develop and mature as a business. I had to empower the team to make decisions and do what was right for the business. I also had to empower the team to challenge me while knowing when I needed to stand strong on certain things as the founder.

I got a lot wrong during this period, and not all the decisions were great. But they were made using the information we had at the time, and we learned some good lessons from the consequences of getting things wrong.

This was an important time for me. I learned about the changes a founder needs to make throughout the evolution of their business to best support it.

Donna moved on in 2017, and was replaced by Faisal. This was a new experience for Sodashi. For the first time we had someone at the helm with experience in both the luxury and cosmetics sector, as well as general management at a CEO level.

Should we have had someone with Faisal's experience sooner? Maybe. But I believe the progression of our GMs matched the organic progression of our business.

Jessica brought not only passion and a nurturing manner to the table, but also a great understanding of the business almost from the beginning. And this created a huge buy-in from all our staff. Donna brought a different management style, and implemented a number of systems and processes.

So when Faisal started he could take a high-level view of our business from both an operations and financial management perspective relatively quickly, and make tweaks to stabilise the business at all levels.

He also empowered me by challenging and educating me, but always in a respectful, progressive and timely manner. And he empowered his line managers by mentoring them and honing their management skills.

Which is why, when we faced the curveball of Faisal wanting to return to Queensland in 2018, we were well placed to give remote management a go. And so far, so good. His line managers in Perth take care of things on the ground while he oversees things from Queensland and comes to Perth for one or two weeks a month.

WHAT THE FUTURE HOLDS

As Sodashi approaches its 20th anniversary, it's been such a treat to reflect on our journey and see how far we've come. It's also been interesting to revisit our values.

LOVE

Sodashi isn't just exceptional ingredients and extraordinarily unique formulas. We put our heart into everything we do and every interaction we have. We strive to create a working environment people love being a part of, and a culture where people can flourish.

INTEGRITY

We always do the right thing—even when it's hard, uncomfortable or inconvenient, and nobody would know any better.

THOUGHTFUL

In every action we aim to be thoughtful, respectful and sensitive. We care how people feel, and consider the impact of our words and actions on others. We aspire to always surprise and delight. Sodashi exists because of its staff, customers, shareholders and suppliers. How we make them feel correlates to our success.

GRACE

We're a small part of something bigger. We remain teachable, and know we don't have all the answers. We serve others and exist for their good as well as our own. We are generous and helpful.

PURITY

We formulate our products using the finest natural ingredients sourced responsibly and sustainably. We stand by the purity of our ingredients, and list them all on the label.

EVOLVING

We're always evolving as a business, as individuals, and as a brand. There are no mistakes, only lessons. We like to ask why and look for better ideas and methods that will move us forward.

NOURISH

At its core, Sodashi is nourishing. We believe that creating skin care in its most natural state, with all the vitamins and minerals and other nutrients intact, is the finest nourishment for beautiful skin. Sodashi is about total health. It goes beyond nourishing the physical body. It nourishes the soul, the senses, the mind and the spirit. Sodashi is alive with the intelligence of nature.

Reflecting on these values, I can say my proudest achievement over the years wasn't *just* building a business that has stayed true to these values. It's having a team I trust implicitly to uphold them.

And really, it's the evolution of that team that most facilitated the important transition I want to talk about now.

the
Founder
Transition

Some people start businesses with the goal of making a difference in the world. They are innovators, and they want to change the status quo.

I'm one of those people.

I wanted to change the way people thought about the products they were applying to their skin. I wanted them to believe that what they put on their skin should be as nutritious as what they put into their bodies.

But I also wanted to ensure the products I created would be effective. I didn't want to be wasting people's time or money. Yes, I wanted the products to be natural. But I also wanted them to make a genuine difference to the skin they were being applied to.

I also wanted to build a company I'd enjoy working in every day. One that would be nurturing, nourishing, purposeful and meaningful.

By 2013 I had ticked all the boxes.

My startup wasn't a startup anymore.

'I had a transition to make—one that's not really talked about much. The transition from 'startup founder' to just 'founder''.

I'd proven there was a market for the Sodashi products. They were being sold in more than 20 countries. We scaled from me making face cream alone in my kitchen to premises in Fremantle that housed our team of 20 and combined our offices and manufacturing facilities. We found international distributors. We had a brand that stood for something, and people understood what that 'something' was.

And so I had a transition to make—one that's not really talked about much. The transition from 'startup founder' to just 'founder'.

When you're a founder in startup mode, you're involved in everything. In the earliest days I was certainly doing it all: formulating, manufacturing, phone answering, accounting, marketing, sales, customer service, training. And it's important to do it all. When you hire people, it's easier to hold them accountable if you understand what their job entails. And it's easier to know if they need any help.

By 2013 (our 14th year of business) I had a strong team in place all doing what they were best at. That meant, at least in in theory, that I could do what I was best at—formulating and building relationships. But I was still too involved in the day-to-day running of the business, and probably becoming a roadblock.

If you're the founder of a startup that's now an established business, here are some thoughts around transitioning your role to one that empowers your teams to do what they do best, and helps your business keep moving forward and growing.

REMEMBER, IT'S HARD TO TRULY STEP OUT IF YOU'RE THERE EVERY DAY

When I was based in Perth I was completely in the loop, which had two effects.

Firstly, I'd poke my nose into stuff I didn't need to simply because I was there.

Secondly, my team would ask my opinion on matters they didn't really need my input on. They knew everything they needed to know, and me being around disempowered them when it came to making decisions.

In the end, it took the drastic step of moving to Sydney for me to step out of the business. If I'd stayed in Perth I wouldn't have been able to stay away from the office. I liked being there and around my team too much.

MAKE SURE YOU COMMUNICATE YOUR KNOWLEDGE PROPERLY

I had to learn to share my knowledge. Not because I'm given to holding things close to my chest to retain control. Quite the opposite in fact. But when I'm busy I forget to share things. It's helped having team members who make it their business to ask questions and get the information out of my head. I often expect people to be mind readers and pick things up from me almost via osmosis, so apologies to all the staff members I've had over the years who had to learn this skill.

Ultimately, you can't transition from startup founder to founder if you haven't transferred what's in your head into the heads of others.

CHECK YOUR EGO AND IDENTITY

When you're a startup founder, you spend so long preserving the brand you gave birth to that it becomes an extension of you.

But you are not your brand. And if you achieve scale and turn your startup into an established business, you'll more than likely have a great team of people around you who will drive the business and ensure its continued success.

Letting go of control is hard. In the end you need to understand what's important to you and let some of the other stuff go. This has been a real benefit to me. I trust the team and enjoy my founder and director responsibilities.

TRY AND GET THE BALANCE RIGHT

Whenever I hired someone, I felt the best thing I could do was help them get up to speed and then leave them to do their job. But I was so paranoid about being seen as a micromanager back then that I stepped away too quickly.

You won't always get this right. But if you're aware of your tendencies, you can improve with each new hire and strike the right balance between:

- ensuring they have the tools and knowledge they need to do their job
- stepping away and trusting them to do that job with minimal input from you.

HIRE PEOPLE WHO CHALLENGE YOU

Founders are determined, fearless innovators and ideas people. They also have great self-belief. These are pretty much prerequisites for the job. However, that combination can sometimes lead to bad ideas being given more air time than they should, or taking the business and the team off on a tangent.

That's why it's important to hire people who challenge you. But they need to be able to do it with respect for both you and the brand. No founder wants to be constantly butting heads with a naysayer in their own company.

It's crucial to have a strong GM and/or CEO in place that you trust. They'll develop, grow and manage your brand. But more importantly they will support you as you support them, with neither of you undermining the other.

I now share my ideas with my GM, and sometimes the management team. And if it's a truly magical idea (as I like to think many of them are), I leave them to do the execution. This way my ideas will be implemented with the proper structure and support from the team.

The final thing to remember when hiring people is that while someone may be a fabulous person, if their vision for the business and the brand doesn't align with yours, or you don't trust them implicitly, it's simply not going to work.

TRY AND GET THE TIMING RIGHT

You'll never do this perfectly. But as I mentioned earlier, if your business isn't a startup anymore then it's time to cut the apron strings and let your team do what they do best (leverage the knowledge they have that you don't) while you do what you do best (the things only the founder can do).

I certainly didn't get the timing of my transition right. But I think that's because when I moved to Sydney I didn't realise that I was leaving behind:

'It's important to hire people who challenge you. But they need to be able to do it with respect for both you and the brand.'

- an office I was used to going to every day

- the ability to be around my Sodashi 'family'

- my network of friends

Adjusting to these while also trying to find my feet in Sydney drew my attention and energy away from the business until I realised what was happening and rectified it.

DON'T LET GO OF THIS ONE THING

While I've said making the founder transition is about letting go and not needing to control everything, there's one thing you can't let go of—the positive attention you have on your business.

People feel that lack of attention and engagement. So much so that when I moved to Sydney and was struggling to hold myself together, people in the industry thought I'd moved on from Sodashi. Not ideal.

UNDERSTAND HOW YOUR ROLE CHANGES

Every founder who makes the transition will experience a change in their role. I take a more 'helicopter' view of things now, but there are five things I still tend to zoom in on:

- **Our company DNA.** I feel I've moved from being embedded in the company's DNA to being its gatekeeper. That DNA is based on the values that were implemented at the very beginning—all-natural ingredients and pure intentions. While our vision has evolved over the years, and will continue to evolve, a primary part of my current role is to ensure we don't stray from our values.

- **Our bank account/cash flow.** I always like to know our

cash position and how we're tracking. This allows me to identify and help the team address potential problems or bottlenecks before they become a real problem.

- **Our products.** A sample of every product we make is sent to me in Sydney.

- **Our vibe.** I'm in Perth every four to six weeks at the moment, and I like to check the atmosphere and environment in the office and our manufacturing. This is super important to a business such as ours that talks about intention.

- **What people are saying about us.** I check in on social media. I like to read the feedback we receive via our international training reports. And I love connecting with our clients.

TRY AND MAINTAIN WHOLENESS THROUGH THE PROCESS

It's important to remember that as the founder you don't just bring technical expertise to your startup. You're a complete person.

This transition is challenging because a large part of your identity is tied to your startup. And when your startup isn't startup anymore, where does that leave you?

This is why, apart from starting the company, this transition may be one of the toughest roles you ever experience.

In any major transition, you've got to find the support you need to help you get through it. It might be talking to a therapist, or having a mentor or business coach. It might be finding a networking or mastermind group. It might be using therapies like meditation, Kinesiology or Bowen therapy. It might be some or even all of these.

But once you get through the transition you'll be liberated, and will likely become more of an asset to your business and your team. You'll get to spend more time working on your business because you're not caught up working in it. Instead of running it you're guiding it, supporting it, caring for it and doing all you can to ensure it's tremendously successful. And you're empowering the entire team to do what they're amazing at because you're really saying, 'I trust you. But I'm also here for you when you need me'.

So keep learning, keep experiencing, keep being inspired and keep growing. Once a founder, always a founder.

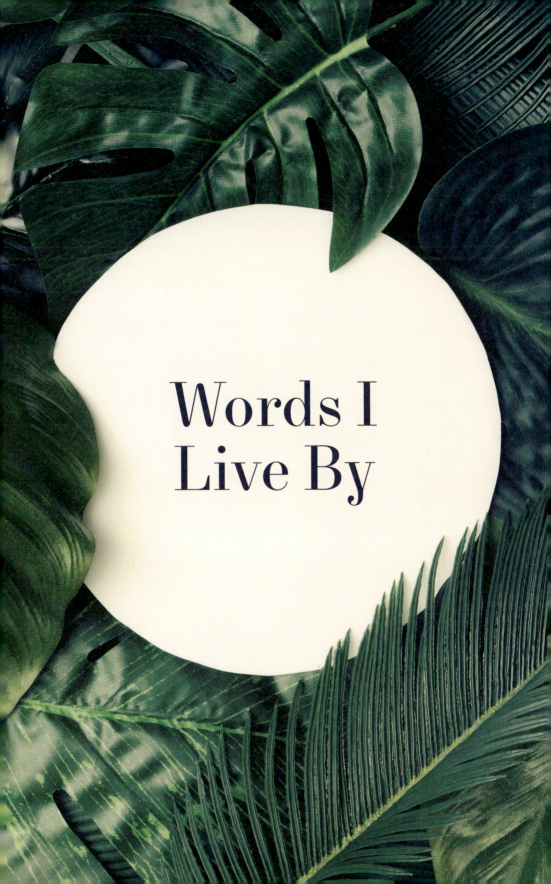

Words I
Live By

I love a good quote as much as the next person, and over the years certain quotes and mantras have resonated with me and helped me on my startup journey. Some of them reflect what I've always thought, while others reflect lessons I've had to learn along the way ...

'If you're not a risk taker you should get the hell out of business.'

– RAY KROC

When you start a business you can create all the spreadsheets in the world and have the best intentions of what your revenue will be for the first couple of years. But if you're relying on those intentions to take the risk out of starting your business then you've got your head in the wrong space.

Every business is a risk.

Which is why you need to ask yourself right from the start, 'How much am I prepared to lose if this goes belly-up?'

> ## 'Be yourself; everyone else is already taken.'
>
> — OSCAR WILDE

Until I started doing my Transcendental Meditation (TM) technique, I don't think I was truly connected to who I really was. I spent a lot of time trying to be the person I (or other people) thought I should be. When I first learned TM my most distinct memory was this feeling of oneness—of being incredibly at peace with myself, and realising that most of the stuff I worried about when comparing myself to others, or trying to be something I wasn't, just didn't matter.

The freedom this afforded me is hard to describe.

> **'Everything we do and everyone we meet is put in our path for a purpose.'**

At the risk of sounding a bit woo, I've always believed my life was mapped out. And because of that, I'm willing to let things unfold rather than always push for what I think should be happening.

While writing this book, it's been interesting to reflect on how that first job at the pharmacy in Napier showed me compounding chemistry and personalising preparations for different skin ailments. How working there gave me a grounding in both skin care and selling. How my work in the hospitality industry gave me an understanding of how hotels worked, both at the front end (customer service) and the back end (accounts, management and administration). Sodashi went on to sell into the hospitality industry, and when I talk to hotel GMs it helps immeasurably that I understand their challenges and can ensure we are providing a real solution.

My mentor also reminded me that my childhood in New Zealand, while not rich in money, was certainly abundant—filled with fresh fruit and vegetables, beautiful home-made clothes, love, nurture and support.

I'm grateful to every person who's had something to teach me along the way.

'I'm not interested in competing with anyone. I hope we all make it.'

— ERICA COOK

About four years into Sodashi I found myself focusing on what other people were doing and comparing myself to them—favourably and unfavourably. It started consuming me, and I had to consciously shift my mindset and tell myself there was plenty of room in the market for all of us and I was best served staying in my own lane.

I could also encourage people on their own journeys.

Zoë Foster-Blake was an Australian beauty editor and went on to create her own unique voice in the beauty industry. Zoë spent years trialling and reviewing beauty products. She and I became friends and would often have conversations about skin care products. In those conversations she suggested approaches and products I felt had merit but weren't suited to the Sodashi brand.

Eventually I said to her, 'Why don't you start your own skin care company?' Her initial reply was, 'Hell no, I don't think I'm up for that'. But a few weeks later she called me and said, 'I've been thinking. I'd like to do it. Can you help me?' I was so thrilled she'd decided to go for it because she had a lot of potential and passion.

Unsurprisingly, Zoë's skin care brand Go-To has gone on to be a great success story.

If I'd seen her as competition I never would have planted the seed and given her my loving support and encouragement. It wouldn't have necessarily stopped her from starting Go-To, but it would have robbed me of the satisfaction of watching her seize an opportunity, grow her wings and make a great success of it.

No matter what industry you're in, there's always more to gain when you collaborate and encourage others, rather than compete with them.

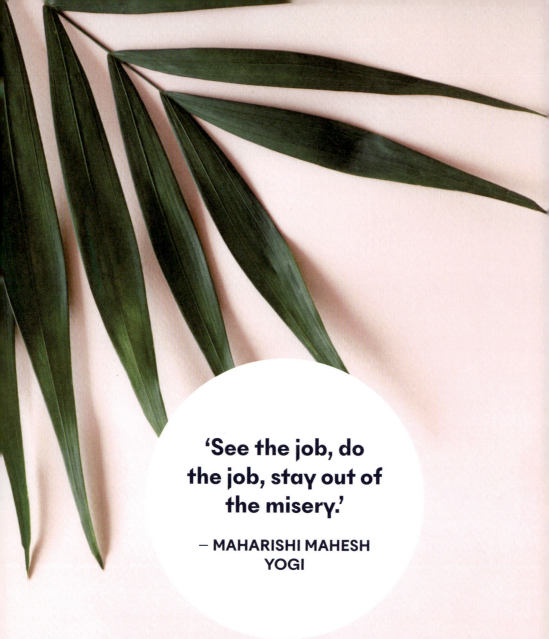

'See the job, do
the job, stay out of
the misery.'

— **MAHARISHI MAHESH
YOGI**

When I keep putting jobs off and not tackling the biggest one first, my energy and attention wanes. But if I pounce on those jobs straight away I feel great. I'm flying, I'm nailing it, and I'm ticking them off my list.

'What's different today than yesterday?'

This is something Ken used to ask me a lot in the early days of Sodashi. And it became a bit of a mantra for whenever I found myself feeling crushed and despondent about something that wasn't worrying me the day before. It may have been that I knew a bit more about the situation. But really, it's no different.

'I am enough.'

When you combine idealism with perfectionism (as I still occasionally do), it can be really hard to cut yourself some slack.

For the first ten years of the business I put a lot of pressure on myself to know everything and be across everything. I always found it embarrassing if I didn't know something. I'd beat myself up, and then double down to ensure I never had to say, 'I don't know'.

It took me a long time to realise I couldn't possibly know everything. Instead I needed to surround myself with people who knew the things I didn't, and fill the knowledge and experience gaps I had. When I finally did that, it took a huge amount of pressure off me. And of course I wished I'd done it earlier because it freed me up to be really good at what I knew rather than passably good at everything.

Today, whenever I need to remind myself of this, I quietly say to myself, 'I am enough'.

'I've learned that people will forget what you said, people will forget what you did, but people will never forget how you made them feel.'

— MAYA ANGELOU

The early years of Sodashi were a grind. I was really going hard and putting so much effort into it. When you're an introvert in that situation, it's easy to retreat into yourself because you're so intensely focused on what you're doing.

In that mode, you don't realise you might seem a bit vague or offhand. And if you don't understand the effect your actions are having on other people, you can lose them very quickly.

I've learned over the years that while you can use a lot of words, when you look at someone's face and realise what you've said or done has affected their day or their life, you need to stop and think about how you've made them feel. And then you need to do something to show you care; that you're not only listening to them but also hearing what they say. That's what people really want—to know you care and are truly listening.

'Everyone is doing the best they can with the resources they have available.'

Even if people aren't necessarily doing their best, approaching the situation with that assumption means you'll come at it with more grace and generosity than if you assume people are trying to hurt you in some way. But the truth is, more often than not people's hearts are in the right place. They just lack execution.

You can also extend this kindness to yourself when you look back on situations you wish you'd handled better. Maturity is a resource. You can think, 'If I had my time again, I'd do things differently'. But the only reason you know what you'd do differently is because you got it wrong in the first place, and grew as a person because of it.

'You can be firm, yet soft.'

This is something I struggled with in the early days. I really avoided having the tough and robust conversations with people. I much preferred being the nurturing one. But then someone reminded me one day that you don't have to be firm and hard. You can set strong boundaries in a soft manner. You can offer firm, constructive feedback but do it softly. It's possible to be firm, yet soft.

'The universe supports your desires, so choose what you desire carefully.'

As a 'big picture' person I've never been a big planner. I'm all for making lists, but ultimately I know wherever I focus my attention is where I'm going to see growth.

This isn't always a good thing. If you focus on something you don't want (and I've seen people do this), you may draw that into your life as well.

But focusing on what I do want, and then having an idea of how I can achieve it, can really pay dividends.

Just under two years ago we were hiring for a new GM at Sodashi. A fellow director and I wrote a list of skills we wanted our new GM to have, as well as a list of what we wanted them to implement and action at Sodashi. We hired our GM, and within a few months it became apparent we'd hired someone who ticked everything on our list.

For this reason, I get those I mentor to write lists of what they want to attract into their lives or businesses. I tell them to be as specific as they can without limiting the outcome. An example I use is, 'If you're looking for a new house, write down an actual street rather than one or two suburbs. Write down how you want the house to look, and even include descriptions and functions of the inside and outside.'

Over the years I've written many lists. Once I write them I usually stick them in a drawer and forget about them. I love finding them (often months or even years later), reading them and reflecting on what I've manifested.

'Right place,
right time, right
people.'

Again, this is going to seem a little bit woo. But I believe that our actions, thoughts and beliefs emit a frequency like a radio station. And the people who tune in to it will be the ones we need to find.

I've felt this resonate many times. And while I can't share every situation when I felt it, there are some standouts:

- When I first met Andrew Stenberg, an Ayurvedic guru. (It was after meeting Andrew and learning about Ayurveda that I knew I wanted to incorporate Ayurvedic philosophies into Sodashi, and have a Sanskrit name.)
- When Anne joined me as the first employee of Sodashi.
- When I first met Robbi and Jim and was introduced to Aroma Tours.
- When Chrissy from Sheraton Bangkok found me at the first and only trade show Sodashi exhibited at.
- When I met the founders and owners of the *Gallivanter's Guide* who've been amazing mentors to me and Sodashi.
- When I first met Nigel Franklyn (aka the Spa Whisperer).
- When Sodashi's external PR consultant, Rachel, became our in-house PR and marketing director.
- When I met Brene Brown and had a speed meeting of five minutes where she said exactly what I needed to hear about being a founder.

One thing I have learned is never to question it. Trust the universe and let things unfold. You'll be amazed what happens when you do.

> **'Genuine relationships are the foundation of every great business.'**

In the early days I was often in a rush because I had so much to do. So I didn't spend as much time with people as I should have, and deep down wanted to. But as things got easier, and I had support and others to help me, I started spending more time with people, investing in them, and really listening to what they were saying.

The hospitality and spa industry (like most industries) is a very small world. Each connection I've established is important to me. When you make the time to create and nurture those connections, good things happen.

I like a challenge. And I like to push myself. But I'm probably no different to a lot of people. I also feel the fear.

These fears can debilitate us. They can also manifest issues for us in our businesses. I've learned that I feel a whole lot better about myself when I push through fears and try not to limit myself.

After having a fear of heights for many years, I climbed the Sydney Harbour Bridge (in the wind and rain as it turned out). I've also ziplined in New Zealand, and now I'm a zipline junkie. Facing and conquering these fears in everyday life has had a brilliant knock-on effect in my business life.

'I'm always doing things I can't do. That's how I get to do them.'

— PABLO PICASSO

> ## 'Perfectionism is self-abuse of the highest order.'
>
> ### — ANNE WILSON SCHAEF

Perfectionism is something I've battled with my whole life. I love this trait when I'm formulating, creating and bringing a new product to market. But it can also get in the way.

Judging yourself constantly is such a bad energy thing. There were times when I spent so much time trying to get something perfect that I missed out on the joy of just doing it, or I missed the joy of something wonderful happening because I was wondering how I could have done it better.

The opposite of perfectionism isn't imperfection. It's self-compassion. Happily, I've had access to some very wise and intuitive practitioners of self-care and self-love over the years, and they've helped me find the self-compassion I need to manage this trait.

For other fellow perfectionists out there I highly recommend another book, *You Are Not Your Brain*.

'Give people time and space to show you who they are.'

As an INFJ (on the Myers-Briggs scale), I'm naturally idealistic. I tend to ignore how people actually are because I'm caught up seeing the person I know they could be. While it sounds nice to see the best in people, it has a downside.

Early on in Sodashi, letting my idealism override my intuition saw me entering into a few relationships too quickly and ignoring what my gut was telling me. And while I learned a lot from those situations, it took me a long time to extricate myself from some relationships. And the process was often harrowing.

Suffice to say, I'm much more tuned in to my intuition than my idealism these days.

> ## 'You must be the change you wish to see in the world.'
>
> **— MAHATMA GANDHI**

For so many years, I'd searched to no avail for a skin care product that didn't make my skin react. I also felt strongly that we shouldn't be putting something *on* our skin that we wouldn't put *in* our bodies.

This was the change I wished to see in the skin care industry: pure, 100% natural, vegan and cruelty-free skin care. And since it was my wish, it was up to me to make it happen. Looking back, this seems quite bold. But at the time, it was the logical next step—one I'm eternally grateful to have taken.

And it's pleasing to me to see that while Sodashi's vision has evolved over the years, we've never strayed from the base philosophy that kicked everything off.

We still use the purest ingredients in the world. And I'm proud that each product continues to be formulated with the utmost care. I love that we've been able to express our company DNA in new ways that create unique value and sustainable advantage while continuing to align the company's strategy to that DNA.

'Innovation distinguishes between a leader and a follower.'

— STEVE JOBS

In the early years I didn't realise how much others needed encouragement to bring their ideas to the table. I had to invite them, and even this could be challenging.

But I learnt that true innovation only takes place when people are given the opportunity to put forward their ideas, take ownership of their ideas and implement them. It won't work if they have to ask permission for every part of the process, or feel they'll be micromanaged in the process. In fact, they will stop asking.

Innovation needs empowerment and an engaged team behind it because it won't work if someone is just going alone. In the same way, if only one person is seen as 'the innovator', it won't inspire others to contribute or bring their innovative ideas forward.

Not every idea will be a flying success. But valuable lessons can be learnt from failure as much as success, and these lessons can be applied to each new attempt. It also provides a safety net for everyone to innovate.

I'm not suggesting you encourage failure. Far from it. But nurturing innovation can ultimately lead to quicker success. I also believe innovation needs to come from the top down to each individual contributor, where senior management and team leaders are involved rather than just mandating a change.

I also like to avoid what I call the roadblocks to implementing innovation. Have a structure to support it, but don't limit innovation by solely focusing on budget, resources and timelines. If you constantly push back on innovation, your company will lose some of its agility and dynamism.

'If your mentors
only tell you that
you're awesome,
it's time to find
other mentors.'

I first came across Lyn Middlehurst in 2003. Lyn and David Maslin
publish *The Gallivanter's Guide*, a monthly 8-16 page publication
created in response to travel newsletters and magazines tending
to gloss over any problems encountered at a property. Lyn and
David's mandate was to 'tell it like it is'.

   And my first experience with Lyn certainly bore that out.

It had just been announced that Six Senses was co-branding with Sodashi, and Lyn started emailing me about the ingredients in the products and asking a lot of questions. She was incredibly passionate about chemical-free natural skin care, and wanted to be certain of our credentials before endorsing the partnership between us and Six Senses in their publication.

Six Senses were quite apologetic about it, but I loved it. I was thrilled someone was taking an interest because I was still having to educate people about the value of pure, effective, natural skin care. To have someone actually asking questions was a huge joy.

I finally got to meet Lyn in person quite by accident. I was in the Maldives visiting a spa, and when I arrived the spa director said to me, 'Lyn Middlehurst is here. I've heard she's had quite a bit of communication with you'.

We all ended up sitting down over lunch and I recall thinking, 'Wow, I can learn so much from her and David'. They'd been critiquing the hotel and spa industry for quite a few years by this stage, and were all about excellence.

I was also excited because here was someone who was as passionate about all-natural skin care as me. While many of our interactions were challenging (Lyn could be very confronting), I kept reminding myself, 'This is the mentor I've been looking for. This is the person who's going to be really honest with me'.

By that stage of Sodashi's development I think a lot of people just wanted me to be successful, so they would tell me the things I wanted to hear. To this day Lyn has only ever told me what I needed to know.

She remains one of my greatest mentors, and a person I turn to whenever I want someone to 'tell it to me straight'.

Self-care

For as long as I can remember I've had an interest in, and awareness around, the need to look after myself. (And remember, that's all self-care is: looking after yourself.)

In my teens I knew *emotional wellbeing* should be my priority, and I would support this via friendships, fun and laughter. Admittedly, I also did the regular pushing of health boundaries the average teenager does. But I did love, and frequently took the opportunity to be with my friends and extended family.

I remember how energising it was when I visited my aunts and cousins in their respective cities in New Zealand. Spending time with them always nurtured and nourished my heart.

When I arrived in Perth in my early 20s, the beautiful weather and outdoor lifestyle the city offered shifted my focus towards my *physical wellbeing*. I started running and playing squash. I really got into the benefits of aerobic exercise because I loved how it made me feel. It was also around this time that I started experimenting with my diet.

Once again, I was ahead of my time here. Today, many people limit their intake of certain foods because they know those things

'Self-care
is simply
the act of
looking after
yourself.'

don't make them feel great. In the late '80s and early '90s, there was little support for the kind of self-experimentation I was doing. All I knew was that certain foods didn't make me feel 'whole' as a person, and others did. I paid attention to what my body was telling me. And if it told me it didn't like something, I'd eliminate it from my diet to see what the effect was. I found it so interesting to note what foods made me feel light and energetic, and which ones affected my ability to focus and concentrate.

By the time I moved to Kununurra, I had some healthy eating and daily exercise practices in place. But the remoteness of that town plus the climate made it difficult to continue those practices. So I just did the best I could. Working in the health food store allowed me to keep learning about what I could do to support my wellbeing from a nutritional point of view.

I also put certain practices in place to support my *mental health*. Each year from December to January I'd take extended holidays that allowed me to go to places where the population was larger and traffic lights were a thing. I particularly loved holidaying in locations that contrasted with Kununurra such as the South Island of New Zealand and a most memorable holiday in Zimbabwe and South Africa. Those trips were essential for my sanity and mental health, and got me through the three years I spent in Western Australia's extreme north.

Moving back to Perth brought with it all the emotional challenges you'd expect from any big change in your life. We'd moved into a new house, I was trying to re-establish myself in the city, and I was doing a job that didn't inspire any passion or purpose in me. Visiting my local health food store during my lunch breaks supported me emotionally during that challenging time, and gave me the confidence and energy I needed to go out on my own.

Taking that step was an interesting one because in owning a health store I was conscious of being a good role model. I see my years at The Health Cottage as some of my best with regard to self-care. You know you're getting the mix right when you feel vibrant, alive and energetic while also having a great capacity to give energy to others. I ticked all those boxes while running The Health Cottage.

And then I went into startup mode with Sodashi.

STARTUPS VS SELF-CARE

A huge amount of personal resources and energy is used in a startup. As you move through the different phases of startup life you're juggling many balls, fighting a to-do list you never get to the bottom of, moving from one meeting to another and dealing with financial pressure while trying to find the energy and space to think clearly and be creative.

It can feel like you're on a rollercoaster. I remember days where my energy was so high I felt I could conquer the world. Unfortunately, they were followed by days where I knew I'd fall in a massive heap if I didn't take the time to regroup and refocus.

When you're driven by passion and purpose it feels like the right kind of energy is fuelling the work you're doing. But then there's the toll that comes from working seven days a week and pushing yourself so hard you're in constant fight-or-flight mode from the adrenaline coursing through your body.

We founders have a tendency to push and push until we collapse. It's only then that we take some time out and recharge. And even then, we only recharge enough to get back on our feet to re-enter the fray.

Before long we're caught in a cycle of pushing ourselves to the brink of collapse, doing *just* enough self-care to stop ourselves from falling in a heap, and then pushing ourselves again.

The problems with this cycle are many.

You're not setting yourself up to make good decisions

Making decisions on the fly and problem solving under pressure can have a serious knock-on effect. Making poor decisions, and then using precious time to deal with the consequences, puts you on a 'bad decision merry-go-round' that can seriously harm your business.

You're not nurturing your relationships

So many relationships are crucial to the success of a startup. If you have a partner or significant other, you really need unwavering support from them.

The relationships you have with your co-founder (if you have one), staff, suppliers, collaborators and customers are all pivotal. And of course, there's also the relationship you have with yourself.

If you're not taking the time to nurture yourself and replenish your energy levels, it's unlikely you'll have the energy to nurture your important relationships, which puts you even further behind the eight ball.

You never get to work *on* your business

All entrepreneurs know the difference between working in their business and working on it. And it's so easy to be consumed by the former at the expense of the latter. We promise ourselves that we'll fix x just as soon as y is taken care of. But then z happens.

'Most successful startups aren't known for what they initially set out to do.'

Before we know it, months have passed and we still haven't addressed x, let alone actioned the innovations needed to move our business forward.

It's hard to change direction

Most successful startups aren't known for what they initially set out to do. At some stage they had to pivot. Twitter started out as a podcasting network. Netflix was originally a mail order DVD service. And PayPal started out as a mechanism to beam IOUs between PalmPilots. (Remember them?)

When I started Sodashi, my intent was to make skin care products for beauty salons. Then came the opportunity for Sodashi products to be used in spas and to create fabulous spa experiences. This was the pivot that took Sodashi global, and also transformed its 'treatment experience'. (We changed from beauty treatments to nurturing and effective spa experiences.)

I wouldn't have noticed that opportunity, much less found the drive and energy needed to make it happen, if I didn't have sound self-care practices in place.

Small problems become big problems

In the previous section I talked about tapping into my intuition and developing my ability to see people for who they are and situations for what they are. I believe this has safeguarded me against having an 'all is lost' moment with Sodashi. The self-care practices I've used throughout my journey have allowed me to notice problems at the smaller/medium end of the scale, and address them before they became giant, business-threatening ones.

These are the reasons I never see self-care as a luxury, but rather as a strong foundation to build on. It's why I always have self-care tools as part of my business toolbox to ensure I'm not running on empty.

When you take the time to use your tools each day to top up your energy reserves, you'll have the energy you need to not only drive yourself, but also take others along on the ride with you.

MY KEY PILLARS OF SELF-CARE

It's so much easier to *maintain* physical, mental, emotional and spiritual good health than to *regain* it. The key is to find a self-care practice that works for you. One that has daily, weekly, monthly and even yearly components you can build routines and habits around and execute with some consistency, even in the face of the daily challenges your business throws at you.

I'll share how to build these self-care routines later. But first I want to share the key pillars of my own self-care practices. These have boosted my resilience and energy over the years, and are the reason I have the same amount of energy for my business today that I did 19 years ago when I first founded Sodashi.

My pillars fall into three rough categories:

1. **The basics.** These are things I strongly feel you should be doing no matter who you are, what you do, or what your economic situation is. They form a very strong foundation of 'looking after yourself' that will allow you to thrive even if you can't put any other self-care strategies in place.

2. **Complementary modalities.** I'm aware these usually involve specialised practitioners. I'm also aware that finances, geography and time might make these unrealistic for many people. But I still want to share what I've found to be incredibly beneficial over the years, and remind you that you can pick and choose the ones that best meet your particular needs and situation.

3. **Things you don't think of as self-care, but are.** Things such as surrounding yourself with good people and accessing sound advice.

THE BASICS

Sleep

Arianna Huffington wrote an excellent book on this topic (*Thrive*), so I won't go into a lot of detail here.

But I need to say this. Sleep is usually one of the first things founders sacrifice when things get hectic. The problem is, when you're not getting enough sleep your body isn't getting the rest it needs to regenerate and repair, and so it's likely your own performance will suffer. You'll be tired and overreactive to situations, and therefore less likely to deal with problems or challenges calmly and objectively.

The fastest way to end this cycle is to prioritise sleep—especially when the going gets tough. Here are the basic principles I follow to get good sleep:

- Set up your bedroom environment optimally (dark, quiet and cool).
- Turn off your screens at least an hour before bedtime.
- Have a set routine for bedtime. I use my skin care routine at night to unwind and relax. Nurturing my skin and myself is one of the last things I do every night.
- Ideally, go to sleep at the same time every night so your body can get into a rhythm.
- Don't eat dinner too late. You should allow at least two hours for digestion before going to bed. Otherwise your body will be trying to digest your food instead of resting.
- Exercise each day.

I aim for eight hours sleep every night. Sleep isn't just good for business performance. It helps you maintain a healthy weight and gives the body and mind time to regenerate and repair.

Eating healthfully and mindfully

Ayurveda is a sophisticated and powerful mind-body health system that originated in India. It made such perfect sense to me when I first encountered it, perhaps because I was blessed to learn a lot from an amazing teacher of Ayurveda, Andrew Stenberg, as well as completing a short course in Ayurveda. (It would be impossible for me to adequately summarise all the Ayurvedic principles in this book. I recommend reading *Perfect Health* by Deepak Chopra if you want to know more.)

Ayurveda isn't just about *what we eat* (although healthy, nutritious food is important). It's also about basic eating and lifestyle principles centred around *supporting and balancing our digestion.*

Digestion is the process of changing the food you eat into a form the body can absorb and use as energy, or to repair and build new tissue. And Ayurveda believes good health starts there.

What impedes digestion? Eating standing up, on the run, or while sitting in front of a computer or television, along with not eating mindfully in a calm or fun-loving environment.

If we're not digesting our food properly, we won't absorb the all-important nutrients from our food that are essential for our wellbeing and vital for our energy and brain power.

Here are my tips for eating to maximise digestion:

- Drink hot water and hot herbal teas.
- Eat freshly cooked foods.
- Take a moment to see and smell your food. (This sets

'If we're not digesting our food properly, we won't absorb the all-important nutrients from our food.'

off nerve impulses that trigger the release of important enzymes to break down your food.)

- Chew your food well and eat at a moderate pace.

- Create a peaceful and relaxed environment to eat.

- Avoid overeating and consuming unhealthy snacks between meals.

When it comes to *what* I eat, I don't believe there's a 'one-size-fits-all' eating plan out there. It's about tuning in to your own body and wellbeing and eating what makes you feel good.

As a founder you're depending on good energy levels and brainpower to make great decisions. And how you lead people is crucial to the success of your business. So consider what foods make you feel your very best. Consider *how you eat*, as well as *how you feel after eating*. Isolate the foods that give you the best sustenance and energy.

It's also important that we never feel deprived, so I adhere to the 80/20 rule, where I make healthy choices 80% of the time. As Dr Libby Weaver states, 'It's what we do consistently that impacts our health and wellbeing, not what we do occasionally'.

These are my 80% basic principles for healthy eating:

- I eat meals made from fresh food.

- I eat green leafy vegetables every day.

- I avoid packaged and processed foods. (This helps me avoid hidden preservatives, additives and sugars.)

- I love herbal teas. Many of these help with digestion, and provide essential nutrients for the skin, hair and nails. I've also found them to be nutritious for my body when under stress or during travel. Some of my favourite herbal teas are nettle, fennel, peppermint, lemongrass, tulsi and dandelion. But I'm also a great fan of the Pukka tea blends.

- I drink around two litres of water a day, preferably filtered and at room temperature. (Icy cold water can interfere with digestion.)

If you're not sure how to construct a healthy eating plan you can use consistently for the rest of your life, consider consulting with an Ayurvedic practitioner or visit Dr Libby Weaver's website (drlibby.com).

Exercise

The physical and mental benefits of exercise are well documented. It supports our digestion and can help us release stress and unwind.

The mental benefits of exercise in particular make it crucial for founders to move their bodies in a meaningful way every day.

My own exercise routine has changed a lot over the years. But I start every morning with a basic yoga routine, which I do for at least 10 minutes. I'm aware that my best habits are created when I stay in a routine. I love yoga for all its health benefits, and as well as being a great stretch for my body I also love that it's portable—I can practise in my own home or anywhere when I'm travelling.

The other lovely by-product of daily exercise is the way it stimulates creativity. I've lost count of the number of tricky problems I've solved, or ideas I've had, when out for a walk, in the gym or on my yoga mat.

Mindfulness

Mindfulness is simply the ability to bring your attention back to the present moment.

'When we think or behave as if we know what someone is going to say, we can miss hearing what they're *really* saying.'

A practical use of mindfulness is when I'm in conversation with someone. As a big picture person, I often find myself drifting off when someone starts getting 'down into the weeds' (deep into details). While I may not believe I need to know what the person is telling me at the level of detail they're offering, I do believe there's a reason I'm in the conversation. If I let my mind wander, I might miss a vital piece of information and then waste someone's time asking them to repeat the information.

I also know that when we think or behave as if we know what someone is going to say, we can miss hearing what they're *really* saying.

Being mindful of my actions—how I respond to someone, something or a situation—has taught me a lot over the years. When I don't like my response to something, it reminds me to address it at my next Kinesiology or mentoring session because I know something is out of balance.

How do I practise mindfulness?

Earlier today I sat in a park and looked at the magnificent blue sky. Then I shifted my attention to the different greens around me—the contrast of the plants, grass, bushes and trees. I noticed the breeze that was ever so slightly cooling. I listened to the voices of the children playing in the park.

If I'm feeling a bit out of sorts I'll often walk out my front door and notice the shadows or patterns on the pavement (something once pointed out by an artist friend). There are always opportunities for mindfulness. And those moments of mindfulness bring a real sense of calm and help centre my days.

COMPLEMENTARY MODALITIES

Transcendental Meditation (TM)

'Transcendental Meditation opens the awareness to the infinite reservoir of energy, creativity, and intelligence that lies deep within everyone.' – Maharishi Mahesh Yogi

I first learned the TM technique 23 years ago. I'd been in the company of some people who had a calm and centred approach to business and life that I really admired. They credited their calmness to their daily TM practice, so I found my way to a TM centre in Perth and attended an introductory lecture. I must admit I wasn't convinced at the time. Interestingly, it was only after having a TM teacher talk to us at an introductory lecture on Ayurveda that I decided, 'Yes, I want to learn this technique'.

And I know the exact day I learned it—11th November 1995.

TM is often dropped in the 'hippie, trippy' category of things I do, but I've never seen it that way. And I have to say that after trying different forms of meditation, the TM technique was refreshingly easy. Unlike other forms of meditation, TM is a mantra-based, effortless technique.

Setting aside 20 minutes twice a day for the practice does take discipline in the beginning. But I've always noticed once people feel the health and general wellbeing benefits, it becomes very easy to set aside that time.

I can do TM on my own (sitting in a chair) or in a group with other TMers. I can do it when travelling (especially on planes), and have found it definitely limits the effects of jet lag.

In business, my mind and surface level can often feel tumultuous, but deep inside is a beautiful sense of calm and centredness. I've lost count of the times TM has helped me make valuable decisions from a place of calm.

I'm not saying I don't get overwhelmed occasionally, or that things don't upset me. But TM (in conjunction with my other self-care practices) does give me the tools and ability to assess and process issues and challenges and bounce back quickly from setbacks.

I'll never forget Jessica, Sodashi's first GM, coming to my office door in 2001 and asking to speak to me. She said that even when everything appeared chaotic and crazy I always exhibited a sense of calm, and she wanted to experience that feeling too.

Jessica's request inspired me to offer all Sodashi staff who'd been with the company for at least three months the opportunity to learn TM. It's always a personal choice if they decide to learn. For the people who have learnt, we get together every afternoon to do a group meditation in the office. I'm such an advocate of this practice; so many of us get the afternoon slump so this is a great pick-me-up. The other benefit is that the Sodashi team members don't go home at night exhausted, so it supports them in their personal lives too. I really missed the Sodashi group TM session each afternoon when I moved to Sydney.

As I write this, one of my stepdaughters has just learned TM and is also doing her final school exams this year. I always love observing someone who has recently learned TM and practises regularly. The benefits are visible in a beautiful and subtle way.

While I practise other acts of self-care, I believe TM is the modality that's provided me with a strong foundation to build on. If you're interested in learning more about TM contact your local certified TM teacher via tm.org.au for Australia, or tm.org if you're international.

THE INVISIBLE EFFECTS OF TM

In 2016 I was nominated for the *InStyle Magazine* Women of Style Beauty Award.

There was a photoshoot, interviews, a Q&A, and then *InStyle* came to my house and shot a short video. All of this would be presented to an esteemed panel of judges who'd decide the winners in each category.

It was wonderful just to be selected as a nominee, but I went on to win the award and it was a total thrill to be recognised for my dedication and commitment to making a difference in the industry and creating natural, safe, nurturing skin care.

While writing this book I came across some of my answers to the Q&A I did for those awards. In there was the question, 'What do you want to achieve in the future?'

I said, 'I'd like to create more beautiful products, working with some new ingredients I haven't used before. But also, something that is really close to my heart is helping other people in business. I'm keen to write a book about my story and my approach to wellness for personal and professional success. With success comes more and more opportunity'.

It blew my mind seeing those words because it's exactly what I'm doing with this book, even though I'd totally forgotten my answers in the interview.

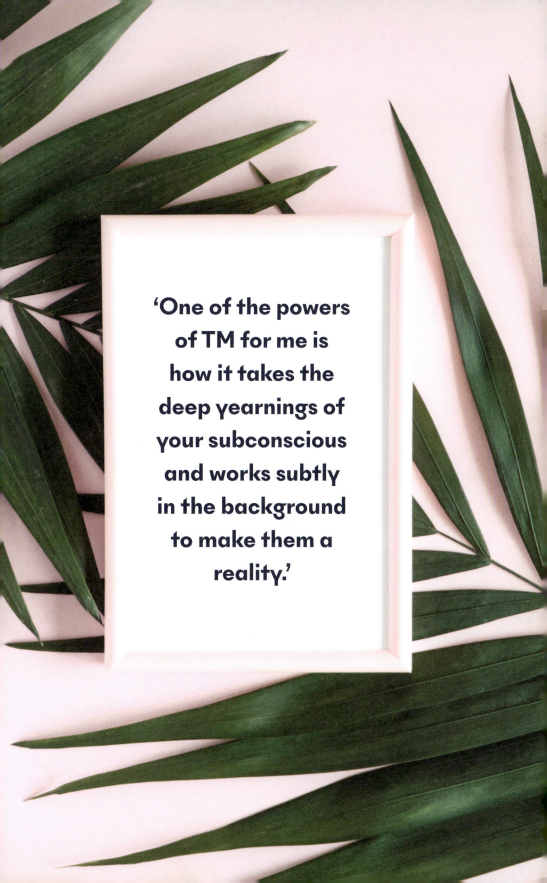

'One of the powers of TM for me is how it takes the deep yearnings of your subconscious and works subtly in the background to make them a reality.'

But that's one of the powers of TM for me. It takes the deep yearnings of your subconscious and works subtly in the background to make them a reality.

———— ● ● ● ————

Kinesiology

Kinesiology is based on the fundamental premise that the body has its own innate healing energy, but sometimes needs help accessing that state.

Kinesiology also recognises there are flows of energy within the body—in our muscles, tissues and organs—all supporting the body to live. Kinesiology evaluates these energy flows by testing the muscles, which reflect the body's overall state of structural, chemical and emotional balance.

I've used Kinesiology for years to address and care for the imbalances in my body's energy. I often refer to my Kinesiology appointment as my 'body tune-up'. While it's very relaxing and comforting, I always feel fabulous after Kinesiology. And I feel it supports the other wellbeing modalities well.

I also use Aromatic Kinesiology, which combines aromatherapy and Kinesiology, and it helps me develop skills and emotional openness to lead a successful, loving and joyful life.

Bowen Technique

This is another holistic, balancing treatment for the body. Bowen restores balance to the body via the autonomic nervous system.

As a startup founder, at times my mind and body were in a high stress state. This meant I was operating on my sympathetic nervous system—the fight-or-flight state. If you spend extended periods in this high stress state, the autonomic nervous system gets overstimulated. While this can lead to other health concerns, it most often appears in disrupted sleep patterns (trouble getting to sleep, trouble staying asleep, insomnia, etc.).

A self-care modality that facilitates rest, relaxation and repair allows healing to occur because you've shifted from sympathetic to parasympathetic dominance.

While I've always practised TM, there were still times where I've experienced very high stress levels. Or I was travelling so much my body was confused about the time zone it was in.

When I have Bowen Technique treatment, it not only alleviates aches and pains but also triggers a deep state of relaxation. My Bowen therapist says it's because my body is releasing stress and shifting to a state of parasympathetic influence.

Acupuncture

Acupuncture is a traditional method of medicine developed over thousands of years in China.

In the body, health relies on the constant circulation of blood to deliver oxygen and nutrients to every tissue, and remove waste materials. Acupuncture plays an important role in regulating circulation in the body.

By inserting fine needles into specific points on the body, acupuncture can release tight muscles, trigger the release of natural pain killers, increase circulation, and regulate the autonomic nervous system (i.e. fight-or-flight, rest and digest, sympathetic/parasympathetic). With these effects, it can treat a wide range of conditions including pain conditions, sleep disorders, digestive issues, and mental/emotional symptoms.

My body benefits greatly from this modality, especially when I combine it with the other self-care modalities I use. Together they really support my wellbeing and allow my body to rest and repair.

Spa treatments

When you're in startup mode every dollar counts. So recommending you spend money on what you may consider an unaffordable luxury may seem completely unreasonable.

But here's the thing. If you're not giving yourself care and attention, you really can't expect to look your best. Stress not only affects us internally, but also affects the health of our skin. While I advocate nurturing and nourishing it every day, a relaxing spa or facial treatment will relax your muscles, support your wellbeing, nourish your skin, and reward you with a healthy glow.

I have a friend who found it hard to justify spending $200 on spa treatments. But she knew how beneficial they were and how great she felt afterwards. So she got a big jar, and now puts all her $1 and $2 coins in the jar. Within two to three months she always has enough in the jar to pay for most of her spa treatment, which she now has at least four times a year.

Because of the industry I'm involved with, I make facials a regular part of my self-care regime, along with regular spa treatments. Consider taking a best friend or your partner with you so you can both relax and spend quality time with each other.

Aromatherapy + Essential Oils

All the way back in 1991, there was a beauty wholesaler in Perth who I could purchase things from because I was a qualified beauty therapist. I remember going in there one day and noticing a small selection of essential oils available for purchase. They were also offering a talk on aromatherapy by a renowned Perth aromatherapist.

I went along to the talk and, as with my first exposure to Ayurveda, what I heard both excited me and made perfect sense.

I remember thinking after the talk, wow, these little bottles of essential oils are medicine for our wellbeing, since they work holistically on the mind, body and emotions.

I immediately immersed myself in learning everything I could about their power and ability to work at those levels to help uplift and restore. What I discovered through my own experience was how wonderful they were for the skin as well.

By 1995 I'd studied aromatherapy and become an educator for one of Australia's leading aromatherapy companies at the time. It was also the year I went to Provence for the first time.

Today, essential oils are still a key foundation of each Sodashi formulation. But while it's important for Sodashi formulations to have a beautiful and natural smell, I've never used essential oils purely for fragrance. Instead I select each essential oil for its specific benefits for the skin.

I love how the physical benefits of the oils in our skin care products are so well augmented by the emotional benefits of a beautiful smelling formulation. Our sense of smell is linked closely with our limbic system (the one responsible for emotions, motivation and memory), which is why aromatherapy can be such a powerful self-care tool.

A SIMPLE
SELF-CARE
ROUTINE
WHEN
TRAVELLING

I've found it even more important to look after myself when travelling. Otherwise I don't have the energy for my business trips, and I return home exhausted and spend too much time recovering. If you travel a lot for work (like I do) it's important to acknowledge that long flights, jet lag, going to meetings straight from the plane, different food and even different drinking water all take their toll.

When I'm on the plane I drink plenty of water. I avoid alcohol, and where possible the plane food. Alcohol is dehydrating, and plane food is hard on my digestion. I usually pack snacks I know my system can digest easily.

I'll also give a plug for a few products I can't travel without. Sodashi's Calming Serum and Eye & Lip Smoother are always in my Ziploc bag so I can apply them regularly throughout the flight. On long hauls I include a cleanser and nourishing cream so I can refresh and revive throughout the flight.

Sodashi's Jetlag Recovery Kit is my biggest friend. Not only does the spray smell amazing, it's an excellent way to refresh and revive yourself. And the jetlag recovery gel is a brilliant pick-me-up that aids my digestion and removes any brain fog. I continue using it for a few days after I arrive.

Once I arrive at my destination I like to do some gentle exercise if it's not too late. A few yoga stretches usually do the trick. However, a walk or a visit to the gym is the ideal way to help the body recover and eliminate any accumulated toxins from the flight.

I also stick to my regular daily self-care routine as much as possible when travelling: my twice-daily meditation, my morning yoga, healthy eating (the 80/20 rule), and cleansing, nourishing and nurturing my skin.

THINGS YOU DON'T THINK OF AS SELF-CARE

Giving yourself permission to be yourself

I remember going to see Arianna Huffington when she was out promoting her book, *Thrive*. She told the story of how for years she would go skiing with her family. Then one day, she realised, 'Hey, I don't actually like skiing. Why am I even going skiing with the family?' At which point she started saying, 'I'll come, but I'm not skiing. I'll do something else while you all do that'.

I just sat there and thought, huh!

As an introvert, I know I need time out and space because that's how I recharge.

I've travelled quite extensively thanks to Sodashi and have been to many amazing cities and destinations around the world. For a long time, I felt I should take advantage of being in these places and explore them while I had the chance. But I often found it exhausting.

Thanks to Arianna, these days I give myself permission to bed down in my hotel room and read a book if that's what I feel like doing. I withhold the temptation to judge myself for all the things I 'should' be doing.

That's not to say I avoid uncomfortable situations or challenges.

For example, my introversion means I really struggle at networking events. It takes a huge amount of energy for me to make small talk with people I don't really know. But I still do it. I just make sure I can get some 'me time' afterwards.

Giving others permission to be themselves

An important part of giving yourself permission to be you is extending the same courtesy to others—giving them permission to be who they are. The world would be a very sad place if we were all the same.

My partner is a huge extrovert who can't walk down the streets of Balmain (where we live) without wanting to talk to everyone. I embrace that side of him in the same way he understands and embraces the side of me that needs to go upstairs and read a book.

Embracing everyone's differences, and working with them instead of fighting against them or expecting everyone to fall into line with how we think or do things, makes you a better leader, partner and person. And it makes both business and personal life easier too.

I like to observe others and notice their characteristics, their behaviours and even how they react to events or circumstances. Being aware of who they are makes it so much easier, because when they do react or behave in a certain way you can accept it because you know that's who they are and what they do.

Developing traits of kindness and understanding will make your journey as a founder so much easier.

Being selective about who sits in the front row of your life

Find your tribe. Take note of the people you hire, the people you spend time with, and even the people you follow on Instagram. Everyone you come into contact with is either giving you energy or taking it from you.

I spoke earlier about feeling like we all operate at a certain level of vibration and resonance, and how we can tune in to it

'There have been many times throughout my business life where I turned to my 'tribe' to support me, listen to me, or simply tell it to me straight.'

and find people at that same vibration. I've also spoken about believing people when they show you who they are.

Surrounding yourself with the right kind of people—people who have your best interests at heart, love you and respect you, but can also challenge you when needed—is a form of self-care that's often ignored.

There have been many times throughout my business life where I turned to my 'tribe' to support me, listen to me, or simply tell it to me straight. There's a lot of wisdom in my tribe, and while I do have a mentor it's my tribe that provides me with snippets of wisdom just when I need them.

Bolstering your self-esteem

Poor self-esteem and self-belief can lead to feeling disempowered when it comes to making your own decisions. It can see you taking advice from people who may not have your best interests at heart. And if you don't believe in yourself, you'll find it hard to push through many of the challenges you'll encounter as a founder.

Working with a mentor or coach who can help you build your self-esteem and self-belief and get in touch with your own voice can be highly beneficial.

For me, my perfectionist tendencies have manifested themselves in some pretty severe self-judgement and self-talk over the years. It's been an important act of self-care for me to learn how to manage this trait.

Both my TM technique and repeating the words, 'I am enough' like a mantra have been key to ensuring I don't tip into 'self-flagellation mode' for failing to see something coming or not getting something quite right.

Having a creative outlet

For me, the formulation side of our products has always been one of my favourite aspects of Sodashi. And it still brings me the greatest joy. But there are many ways to express yourself creatively:

- Solving problems is creative.
- Finding a new way to do something is creative.
- Tinkering with a recipe is creative.
- Gardening is creative.
- Colouring in is creative.

I've always believed that having a creative outlet is an incredible act of self-care. And it doesn't need to involve some big and wild artistic expression. It can often be found in the simplest of things.

Having good financial management practices

Few things in life or business cause more stress than financial instability and uncertainty. At several points in the Sodashi journey I lost sleep worrying about being able to pay our staff and fretting over cash flow problems.

While some of these situations are unavoidable and simply part of growing a business, many can be avoided by having strong financial management practices. As the founder, cash is something I keep my eye on constantly.

Every founder needs someone who will strongly manage the company finances. For self-care and health reasons you need a finance manager you can trust—someone who'll work with you or your GM to ensure the company is in a healthy financial position. It's helped Sodashi a lot to have an experienced GM to manage growth and ensure that when we expand our operations it isn't done at a speed that threatens the viability of the business.

Having a mentor

As I mentioned, my 'tribe' provides me with wisdom, life experiences and knowledge. So I feel I have many mentors.

But I also always have a dedicated mentor—someone I pay monthly who, amongst other things, knows my goals and aspirations and holds me accountable to achieving them.

A mentor is someone you'll develop a relationship with and who should be your trusted guide. You'll feel comfortable sharing your short and long-term goals and aspirations as well as your vulnerabilities. They will help you see the beautiful qualities, hope and wisdom inside yourself.

They will also guide, listen, motivate, uplift, inspire, encourage and support you. And they'll be genuinely interested in you and your questions and concerns.

There are many different mentors available. I recommend finding one who is a good fit for both your needs and your personality.

Making time to refresh your soul

My favourite place to refresh my soul is in the heart of Provence in the South of France, amongst the lavender fields in bloom.

But we don't have to travel to exotic locations to refresh our souls. All we need to do is prioritise taking a refreshing break each year. Ideally this break should be a happy place for you; it doesn't need to be far from where you live. I feel refreshed when I'm in nature and amongst trees, plants, mountains and water.

I have friends who simply like to retreat somewhere to read, rest and relax, or go away and have quality time with their children.

In the early years of Sodashi I'd often be taken away for surprise weekends. I recall how refreshing and restorative this was, and how I'd return to work feeling re-energised and filled with well-thought-out ideas.

This year, for the first time, I went entirely off the grid. I disconnected myself from all communication (including my phone and the internet) for six days to cruise, hike and explore the beautiful surrounds of the South Island of New Zealand. I was entirely refreshed by the beauty and nature that surrounded me for six days, as well as the love of my close family who were with me.

Skin care

While my bias is evident in this regard, I feel strongly that looking after our skin is a crucial aspect of self-care. Our skin is our largest organ, and protects us against exposure to anything dangerous in the environment (such as bacteria) while also protecting our important underlying structures (blood vessels, nerves and organs).

From a cosmetic point of view, I know people are always looking for a magic cream that will wipe away years of neglect. While I've created creams that reverse some neglect, I've always believed we should nurture our skin from both the inside out and the outside in every day.

Our skin is such a great barometer for how well we're looking after ourselves. When I've been travelling too much, or pushing myself too hard, it always shows up there first.

And when I'm eating well, moving every day, getting good sleep and drinking lots of water, my skin glows. And when my skin glows I feel great about myself.

I love the fact that, as a rule, if you're doing things that lead to great skin, you're also doing the things you need to look after your entire body.

A SIMPLE SKIN CARE ROUTINE

I was 13 when my mother bought me my first cleanser and moisturiser. And I can't recall a day since that I haven't cleansed and moisturised my skin.

If you're eating well, moving every day, getting good sleep and drinking lots of water, your daily skin care routine doesn't need to be complicated. Here's all you need to do:

- CLEANSE your skin morning and night. A gentle, creamy cleanser will help remove excess oil, dead skin cells, pollution and makeup. It also helps prevent blemishes and breakouts, and balances the oils your skin naturally secretes.

- MOISTURISE in the morning to help maintain the skin's moisture and hydration through the day.

- NOURISH at night with a face oil (serum) or rich cream to help repair and regenerate the skin.

BUILDING AN ONGOING SELF-CARE PRACTICE

It's one thing to understand that ongoing self-care is crucial for both you as the founder and the long-term success of your business. It's quite another to put it into practice.

As mentioned earlier, the pattern I tend to see is people working themselves into a situation where they completely burn themselves out. Or experiencing a breakdown brought on by severe depression and anxiety. Only then do they think about what they could/should be doing to look after themselves. It's almost as if they have to push themselves to the brink before they can justify self-care.

I so want to challenge this mindset.

I want founders to stop looking at self-care as something to remediate a breakdown or complete exhaustion. I want them to create an ongoing practice *now* with a view to creating energy levels that can sustain them consistently every day.

Of the self-care modalities I shared earlier, the non-negotiables for every person (founder or not) are:

- Sleep
- Nutrition
- Exercise
- Mindfulness

If these form the base of your self-care routines and habits, you'll always be well supported.

To help you give these things the priority they need, I'd love

SLEEP

How will the right quality and quantity of sleep help me function better personally and professionally? _____

_____

_____

How many hours of sleep do I need to thrive (not just survive)?

_____

What time do I need to go to sleep each night to get that number of hours? _____

What barriers are currently stopping me getting to bed at that time? _____

_____

What can I do to remove those barriers? _____

_____

Is there anything affecting the quality of sleep I'm getting?

_____

What support do I need to address these issues? _____

_____

What is my plan for getting the right quality and quantity of sleep going forward? _____

_____

_____

NUTRITION

Why is it important for me to eat a diet that's nutritionally sound?

_____

_____

_____

What is my diet like right now? _____

_____

_____

What do I need to change? _____

_____

_____

What support do I need to make these changes? _____

_____

_____

What is my plan for eating three nutritionally sound meals each day?

_____

_____

_____

_____

_____

EXERCISE

Why is exercise important for me? _____

_____

_____

How much exercise am I currently getting? _____

_____

Is this enough to boost my physical and mental energy each day?

_____

If not, what are the barriers stopping me from getting the exercise
I need? _____

_____

What can I do to remove those barriers? _____

_____

Do I need extra support or accountability? _____

_____

What is my plan for getting the right amount of exercise going
forward? _____

_____

_____

_____

_____

MINDFULNESS

Why is it important to find moments in each day to quieten my mind
and just 'be'? _____

_____

_____

_____

Do I currently have any of these moments in my day? _____

_____

_____

If no, what can I do to find these moments? _____

_____

_____

_____

_____

_____

_____

_____

_____

_____

_____

SUMMARY

What will my daily non-negotiables be when it comes to self-care?

_____

_____

_____

_____

_____

_____

_____

_____

_____

_____

_____

_____

_____

_____

_____

_____

Once you have these 'non-negotiable' routines and habits in place, you can start adding other modalities. And it's totally up to you to decide what those modalities are. The only important thing is to be intentional and focused about creating the time you need to implement them.

Remember, no-one will give you the hour you need to get a massage, go for a walk, or have a nice meal with a friend. Those segments of time need to be carved out.

If you're struggling to find those segments of time, then chances are you're hopelessly overcommitted and need to start saying 'No' to things you really don't need to be doing. (This is Boundary Setting 101, and while it might be hard at the start it will get easier once you start reaping the benefits of committing more time to self-care activities.)

It's now time to build a wider self-care plan—one with daily, weekly, monthly, quarterly and yearly components.

For example, here's my current plan:

DAILY – Meditate for 2 x 20 minutes. Eat nutritionally sound meals. Move my body for at least 15 minutes. Sleep for 7-8 hours. Cleanse, nourish and nurture my skin twice a day.

WEEKLY – Take some time each weekend to rest, relax and read. Go to the gym or do yoga 3-4 times a week. Have meaningful catch ups with my partner and close friends. Have at least one 'at home' facial.

MONTHLY – Have two one-hour calls with my mentor. Have a facial or spa treatment. Have an acupuncture session and a Bowen Therapy treatment.

QUARTERLY – Make a Kinesiology appointment.

Spend a weekend away from the city, preferably in nature with my partner, close friends or in New Zealand with my family.

YEARLY – Spend two weeks holidaying with my partner. Spend Christmas with my family in New Zealand. Go to Provence for 7-10 days. Never work on my birthday.

NOW LET'S CREATE YOUR PLAN:

DAILY – _____

_____

_____

_____

WEEKLY – _____

_____

_____

_____

MONTHLY – _____

_____

_____

_____

QUARTERLY – _____

_____

_____

YEARLY – _____

_____

_____

Please don't take an all-or-nothing approach to the execution of this plan.

If there's one thing I've learned from working with my mentoring clients, it's that nothing gets done without a plan in place. *But* you also need to be realistic and flexible. Because life does happen.

Create your plan, and if it needs tweaking in the future to account for changes in your circumstances or priorities, make the tweaks.

After a month of executing your plan, I'd love you to come back to this book and work through these reflection questions.

SELF-CARE PLAN REFLECTION QUESTIONS

Take some time to reflect on these questions once you've put your self-care plan in place and have been executing it for a month or so.

Do I feel different, or am I performing differently now, compared to a month ago? **YES NO**

If yes, in what way? (Tick all that apply)

O Greater patience   O Greater resilience

O More centred and connected   O Calmer

O Higher levels of creativity   O More energy

O More clear-headed   O Improved decisions

O Improved relationships

Do I need to tweak my self-care plan?   **YES NO**

In what way?_____

_____

Do I need more support from the people around me? What kind
of support? _____

_____

_____

Do I need more time to nurture and nourish my personal
relationships? If so, how will I create that time? _____

_____

_____

_____

Do I need more support from myself? What can I do to give
myself the support I need? _____

_____

_____

_____

What is my measure of self-care success? _____

_____

_____

_____

What can I do to ensure I achieve that goal in the next 30 days?

_____

_____

_____

_____

_____

Conclusion

About 18 months before I started writing this book I was interviewed by *Elle* magazine for a feature. One of the questions they asked was, 'What was your I-think-I've-made-it moment?'

My response?

'Ha ha. I think I'm still waiting for it'.

The beauty of writing a book is it forces you to reflect on where you started, the challenges you've faced, and where you've gotten to.

This is where I've gotten to:

- I've formulated and put into the market more than 200 products that are dominant in the high-end spa industry.

- I've enabled and driven a culture shift in the beauty industry. What we pioneered with Sodashi has started to become mainstream. More and more people are demanding natural skin care, or transparency in ingredients.

- I've facilitated hundreds of thousands of treatments that are impactful, transformative and nurturing around the globe.

- I've created a shift in work culture–from a movement where employers only take from employees to one where employees are supported holistically and mindfully.

- I've created a business that has supported more than 70 people to learn the Transcendental Meditation technique and given them the opportunity to practise that technique every day.

- I've inspired people to stick to their value-driven dreams, and follow their passion and purpose.

- The business I founded now exports safe, natural and effective skin care to more than 25 countries around the world. And all out of Perth, the most isolated capital city in the world.

It was an interesting exercise compiling that list. When you're a founder you tend to be very forward-focused. When you're leading a team, you're very aware there's no 'I' in 'team'. So you never stop to take stock of how far you've come or give yourself credit for what you've achieved.

Which means you're neglecting one crucial pillar of self-care I didn't mention in the previous section–acknowledging how much you've grown as a person and noting the strong foundations you've built from which future growth can spring.

I feel truly blessed and grateful because writing this book has forced me to do this reflection. And if I was asked, 'What was your I-think-I've-made-it moment?' today, I can now answer, 'Writing this book'.

Thank you for coming on this journey with me.

My hope is my story and learnings have inspired you to:

- Pursue your value-driven dreams.

- Follow your passion and purpose in life.

- Take the time to nurture and look after yourself along the way.

- Build your business and life from a place of sustained energy and vitality.

My journey doesn't end here, of course. My life and business will keep unfolding and evolving with the support of the self-care mechanisms I've put in place. I look forward to your journey unfolding in the same way.

Stay in touch

If you'd like to find out more about me or get in touch, you can contact me via:

- **My website:** meganlarsen.com.au
- **Instagram:** instagram.com/megankaylarsen
- **Twitter:** twitter.com/megankaylarsen

If you enjoyed the story of Sodashi, you can find out more about our products and the intention behind them at sodashi.com.au.

You can also keep in touch via:

- **Facebook:** facebook.com/sodashiskincare
- **Instagram:** instagram.com/sodashiskincare
- **Twitter:** twitter.com/SodashiSkinCare
- **Pinterest:** pinterest.com.au/sodashi

Acknowledgements

When I decided to write this book, I had no idea what it would take and what I would learn through the experience. I'm now in awe of every author who has made the same decision.

I also have many people to thank, not only in relation to the book, but also for all the support they've provided to me over the years.

First, a gigantic heartfelt thank you to my editor Kelly Exeter. You worked above and beyond to get this book to print. Your refinement, finessing and awesome project management made writing my first book both possible and an incredible experience.

Thanks also to Kelly's team of Bill Harper (line editor), Kym Campradt (proof reader) and Swish Design (interior book design), along with Jacqui Porter from Northwood Green for her work on the cover.

My love, grace and gratitude also go to:

- **Paul.** You make me laugh every day, you challenge me, and you remind me to live in the moment. I love each adventure we have together. Writing this book was a whole lot easier because of your love, support and encouragement.

- **Mum.** For your unconditional love, for being a pillar of strength, for teaching me the gifts of resilience, humility, kindness and generosity, as well as the importance of keeping my feet firmly on the ground.

- **My darling nieces, Analeise and Sophia.** You have no idea how much your humour, talent, love and spirited fun have supported me through times of stress. You make me feel like the most adored aunt on the planet.

- **My six stepchildren.** Each one of you has a special place in my heart. Thank you for your inspiration, your teachings, your love, your trust and especially your understanding.

- **The Sodashi team.** For trusting me and at times going along with my crazy ideas or challenging the ones that were too crazy. For all your belief and passion in Sodashi, and especially for all your nurturing, care and support to make it the amazing company it is.

Thanks also to everyone I mentioned in this book as well as my dear family, friends, and everyone who has inspired, supported or had something to teach me on my journey.

Finally, there are others who hold a special place in my heart (and you know who you are). Thank you for your love, care, inspiration, nurturing and for being genuinely excited I was writing a book. You are the best tribe a girl could ask for.